Tewdric
of Wales

Tewdric
of Wales

Saint, King, Warrior, Martyr

A. R. UTTING

THE CHOIR PRESS

First published in the United Kingdom in 2020 by
The Choir Press

ISBN 9178-1-78963-096-1

Contents

Preface

The village name of Mathern is a probable contraction of the Welsh 'Merthyr Brenin', which translates as 'The Place of the Martyred King'. This king's name was Tewdric. Few people have ever heard of him, even in Wales, but if he had not fought, and died, for his kingdom, driving off a 'Saxon' invasion at Tintern on the River Wye, it might well have become incorporated into Anglian Mercia. This, likewise, is not appreciated. Tewdric had ruled well. His kingdom was at peace, his laws good, and his people prosperous. Although he died as the result of a head wound sustained in the battle, he left his son Meurig a realm strong enough to resist successfully any further Anglian incursion for at least thirty years thereafter.

Between them they may be said to have laid the foundations of Wales. Urban, Bishop of Llandaff (1119–1129) confirmed that the 'Manor of Merthyr Tewdric (*The Matyrdom of Tewdric*) was truly of ancient British origin. King Meurig married a lady named Onbrawst, a princess of the Ircingas whose kingdom occupied much of what is now Herefordshire, thus securing diplomatic influence beyond his own frontiers. His name endures to our own day, not just as a personal Welsh name, but in Pwllmeyric (*The well of Meurig*) a village to the west of Chepstow. Mathern, where St Tewdric is buried in an ancient church dedicated to him, is a mile or so further on towards the River Severn. How this came about is explained later in this book. The dynasty endured until around 1070 when the Normans effectively swept it away following their conquest.

One of Meurig's sons was called Arthwyr, or perhaps Arthrwys, which circumstance has caused a deal of wishful thinking about possible connections with 'King' Arthur of the Round Table fame. Indeed, during the 1980s and '90s there were periodic romantic claims from Arthurian enthusiasts, both local and from around the globe, that the truth of the Arthurian legends had been as good as established. To put this enthusiasm for all things Arthurian into some sort of historical perspective, I wrote two little booklets, "Tewdric – Saint and Warrior King" (1988) and "Who Slew Tewdric?" (1998). My efforts were not always regarded as praiseworthy, though, and my then teenaged daughter even broke into verse:-

"Oh help!!!!
He's back!!!
He's haunting us, that tale we've come to dread
How can a hairy hermit so turn a Saxon's head?
He lived a thousand years ago, of this we can be sure.
But now he's dead and buried under the chancel floor.

The rest of his life's shadowy – a tale passed down the years.
We've heard it time and time again, it's driving us to tears!
We've nothing personal 'gainst King T, the Celt of many a fad.
It's more the ideas tried on us by our dear old Saxon Dad.

The family has heard the tale; likewise have visiting friends
Plus hordes of 'interested' villagers . . . a list that never ends.
A blaze of printed booklets haunts Britain's fair green hills,
From mountain moors and heathlands to bubbling, rippling rills.

We wouldn't mind so very much our Saint's promoted fame
If every time the tale was told the story stayed the same!
Perhaps it is the mixture of mulled and blended wine,
That sparks the subtle changing of this story passed through time.

Old Tewdric haunts the nave at night to scare the bats away
Which leaves him tired and crotchety, so he sleeps through the day.
But how can he sleep well if you spout history like a pest?
So come away, dear Saxon, and leave him to his rest."

(Rebecca Utting, circa 1995)

Indeed, from time to time I have acted as something of a 'long-stop' to enquiries about Tewdric. I have also lectured on him to groups of people visiting his church, ranging from serious academics to inquisitive Brownies. But now I have finally been spurred to purposeful activity by a good old friend and former colleague who buttoned-holed me and spoke spoke thus; "You know, you really ought to combine your little books on Tewdric into something a bit more *definitive* before you die." Well, put like that, what could I do but try to ensure our local Dark Ages' Saint and King his due fame for posterity?

I soon found that a number of well qualified people had done much careful and serious work on the so-called 'Dark Ages' since last I had delved into them in the1990s. I had plenty of reading to do, and a deal of up-to-date thoughts to think as a result. What follows is the outcome of my efforts. I do not for a moment claim they are definitive, but the story has certainly not quite "... stayed the same ..." and I hope it will both entertain, and also inspire careful research by suitably qualified specialists. The 'Dark Ages' were, frankly, what might happen to us tomorrow if all the wretched IT gadgets upon which we over-depend these days were to run out out of batteries. And no more than that. People got on with life; they had no option. And those who coped really well became famous. Please read on ...

A R (Tony) Utting. October 2019

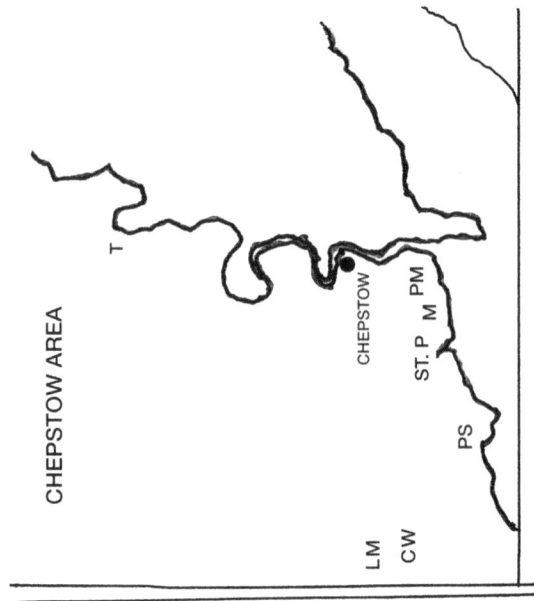

CHEPSTOW AREA

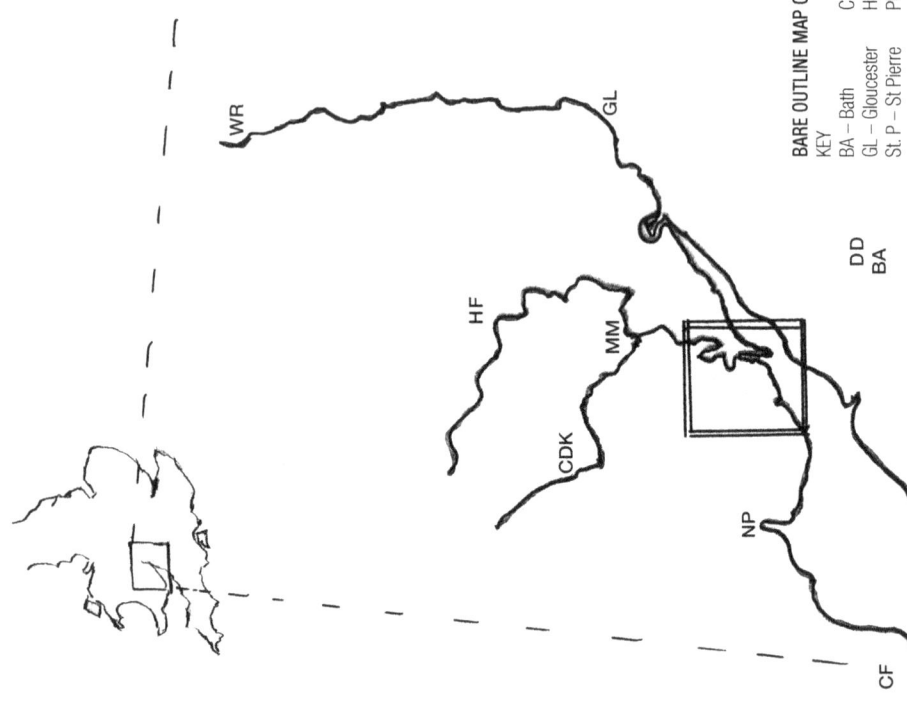

BARE OUTLINE MAP OF PLACES MENTIONED IN THE MAIN TEXT
KEY

BA – Bath	CDK – Clodock	CF – Cardiff/Llandaff	CR – Cirencester	CW – Caerwent	DD – Dyrham Down
GL – Gloucester	HF – Hereford	LM – Llanmelin Fort	M – Mathern	MM – Monmouth	OX – Oxford
St. P – St Pierre	PM – Pwllmeyric	PS – Portskewett	SL – Stoke Lyne	T – Tintern	WR – Worcester

1

The Tale of Tewdric

Who was Tewdric?

In the 'Liber Landavensis' – the Book of Llandaff – we read:-

"King Tewdric when he was in his kingdom enjoying peace and administering justice to his people, had less regard for temporal than for eternal power, and accordingly gave up his kingdom to his son Meurig, and commenced leading an eremitical life amongst the rocks of Tintern (*heremitalem in rupibus Dyndirn*). When he was there resident the Saxons began to invade his land against his son, Meurig, so that unless he individually would afford his assistance, his son would be altogether dispossessed by foreigners. Concerning which, Tewdric said that whilst he possessed his kingdom, he was never overcome but always victorious; so that when his face was seen in battle the enemy immediately were turned to flight.

"And the angel of the Lord said to him on the preceding night, 'Go tomorrow to assist the people of God against the enemies of the Church of Christ, and the enemy will turn their face in flight as far as Pwll Brochwael *(Brockweir?);* and thou being armed, stand in the battle, and seeing thy face and knowing it they will, as usual, betake themselves to flight, and afterwards for the space of thirty years in the time of thy son, they will not dare to invade the country; and the natives and other inhabitants will be in quiet peace, but thou wilt be wounded by a single stroke in the district of Rhyd Tintern, and in three days die in peace (*et tu tamen vulnerabis una plaga in Ryd Ttindyrn et morieris in pace post triduum*).'

"And rising in the morning, when the enemy of his son Meurig came, he mounted his horse and went cheerfully with them, agreeably to the commandment of the angel; and being armed, he stood in the battle on the banks of the Wye near the ford of Tintern; and his face being seen, the enemy turned their backs and betook them to flight; but one of them threw a lance, and wounded him therewith, as had been foretold him; and he therefore rejoiced, as if spoil had been taken on the vanquishing of an enemy. After his son Meurig returned victorious, and with the spoil that he had taken, he requested his father to come with him, who said thus, 'I will not depart hence until my Lord Jesus Christ shall bring me to the place which I have desired, where I shall like to lie after death, that is, the island of Echni (*Flat Holm?*).' And early in the morning two stags, yoked and ready, were before the house where he lodged, and the man of God knowing that God had sent them, mounted the carriage, and wheresoever they rested, there fountains flowed, until they came to a place towards the Severn. And when they came there a very clear fountain flowed, and the carriage was completely broken, he then commended his spirit to God, and ordered the stags to depart; and having remained there alone, after a short space of time, he expired.

"His son Meurig being informed of the death of his father, built there an oratory and a cemetery, which were consecrated by by St. Oudoceus (*Euddogwy*); and for the soul of his father he granted the whole territory to Bishop Oudoceus, and the church of Llandaff, and its pastors in perpetual consecration without any payment to any mortal man besides St Oudoceus and the Church of Llandaff."

There follows a very detailed description of the (then) Mathern Parish boundary, which still aligns with the present boundary to a fair extent and can be followed without too much uncertainty or conjecture. The difference between the two would seem to be on account of endowments having been made subsequently from the area specified for founding the parishes of Chepstow and St Pierre. Undoubtedly the whole point of recording the Parish boundary as part of the Tale was to ensure that the See of Llandaff had a clear and apparently ancient record of its lands, and was thus able to obtain all rents and payments due to it. It is important to remember that the Book of Llandaff was written a good five hundred years after Tewdric's battle and subsequent events took place, and therefore should not be regarded as an eye-witness account of them.

The same is true of the other Tewdric entry in the Book of Llandaff, which occurs in a reference to St. Teilo, "... during whose life the Church of Llandaff, through his sanctity in conduct as well as in doctrine, increased in churches and lands which were given to it, with all their liberty, dignity, and privilege, by his contemporary kings: – Tewdric ap Teithfallt, Iddon ap Ynyr Gwent, Gwrgan Mawr, Maelgwn, Aircol Lawhir, Cadwgan, Tredecil, Rhun ..." and many others, all – or some – of whom may have had dealings with the early Church in Wales, but whose inclusion in this list simply piles on the evidence for its being an hilarious forgery. A parallel case in our own day would be a document signed by the Prime Minister and having as its 'witnesses': – Sir Winston Churchill, Oliver Cromwell, Lady Gaga, Mother Theresa, Neils Bohr, Elvis Presley, Sherlock Holmes, General Eisenhower, Sir John Falstaf, ... and as many other 'celebrities' as would be recognised by the casual reader, all presented in this context as eminent contemporary witnesses of impeccable character adding the lustre of perfect integrity to the document. It had not occurred to the clerk writing this entry in the Book of Llandaff that a list of famous names did not automatically make a dubious or contrived claim for money due to Llandaff a good one.

Also we must recall that the Book of Llandaff is concerned primarily with the life and deeds of St Teilo, who was claimed by Llandaff as its founder. He is also credited with having founded perhaps twenty other churches and religious houses. When the saint died, two of these in addition to Llandaff wanted the honour (and the proceeds from pilgrims, no doubt) of providing his final resting place. In the event this proved to be no problem; the saint's corpse miraculously triplicated itself, we are told, thereby enabling every church which wanted a dead St Teilo to inter to bury one. Llandaff, of course, claimed it possessed the best body, and wrote the Book of Llandaff to underline the superior status that this afforded it.

As the late Canon E T Davies points out in his history of Mathern, the

Book of Llandaff reflects the first half of the twelfth century, when it was written, far better than the sixth century which is its ostensible subject matter. We had better, therefore, consider briefly the cultural/political background to the Book of Llandaff's creation before attempting to extract from it worthwhile information on Tewdric and his times. Very little about the sixth century is entirely certain.

It is worth recalling that up to the Norman conquest, and for a long time after it, the Welsh were a distinct political entity and lived under their own princes, governed by their own laws. There was certainly a recognition that for all practical purposes the kings of England were a superior power beyond the Severn Sea and Offa's Dyke, but relations between the two countries were generally amicable, and the question of suzerainty unspoken and, essentially, unmentionable in the interests of good neighbourliness. By the mid 11th century, though, there was new pressure from the English. Earl Harold Godwinesson (who lost a rather important battle near Hastings in 1066) had earlier come raiding across the border, and there was a sense of all parties chafing at the status quo.

Next the Normans/Norsemen, as their name suggests – best viewed as Vikings who had settled in France and picked up a little polite social polish, if only for such occasions as it was likely to be to their advantage – arrived on the scene. It was soon clear to them that Wales had potential worthy of their interest, and was therefore ripe for conquest and exploitation. With the Norman land seizure came Norman (feudal) administration and, since literacy and book-keeping were chiefly priestly (clerical) arts, there came into Wales the Norman Church, to modify, take over, and replace the existing 'Celtic' church arrangements. This meant that Welsh lands and revenues went to support the new order. For day-to-day purposes the change can have been scarcely noticeable, but it would have been felt keenly amongst the middle-ranking clergy whose promotion prospects and influence were thereby diminished by a new set of 'foreigners' at the top of the Church hierarchy. We may be sure that there was grim objection, if muted, to Welsh revenues going outside Wales to finance foreign bishops or abbots and their mother churches and monastic foundations. These, let it be recalled, could just as easily have been in France as in England.

A dislike of being required to provide support for alien institutions in Europe is nothing new within these shores.

Accordingly a native 12th century Welsh churchman, knowing that his own tradition of Christianity might just possibly stretch back unbroken from Roman times, would consider that he had a long-established claim to all donations made over the centuries to his Church. Thus he would cite every conceivable benefactor both confirmed and and conjectural (or entirely mythical in some cases) as proof of his title in the face of claims made by intruding Normans, both clerical and lay. But he would also make common cause with a fellow, though Norman, Churchman if it appeared to him that any church property was about to be grabbed by some parvenu Norman knight, and in such a case be noisily certain that it would be much better stewarded in the hands of mother Church. Therefore records of the Welsh Church's right to all its incomes were compiled from every possible source. Such considerations undoubtedly shape the Book of Llandaff, as we have seen with the 'king list' associated with St Teilo. Could they also colour Tewdric's tale a little?

They might. We have noted that the Mathern parish boundaries are as carefully noted in The Book of Llandaff as is the account of Tewdric's life and death. It also makes much of Tintern as the place of his hermitage. In other words, the Church approves of him, and takes especial care to mention that he was resident as a hermit at Tintern some 500 or so years earlier than the (French) Cistercian monks. They began building the first version of their abbey there on (appropriated Celtic Church hermitage?) land granted to them in 1131 by (the Norman) Walter fitz Richard de Clare. The Book of Llandaff is reckoned to have been written 1130–1155 in the form in which we now have it, and Welsh churchmen might have viewed the collective foreignness of Tintern Abbey's foundation as three alien wrongs done to their predecessors and their nation, namely the appropriation of the setting of Tewdric's hermitage, a wrongful land grant thus made, and the indignity of these thing having come to pass as the result of military conquest.

Tintern is located upon the Welsh-English border. The name probably derives from 'Dinas y Brenin' – the king's fortress. Whether or not the name was current in Tewdric's day we cannot say, but we have a choice of two Iron Age forts on the hills west of the river Wye, one south of the present abbey and village, and the other, which is the larger, somewhat to the west. Possibly one or the other of these gave rise to the name. Archaeology suggests that there was a small Romano – British farm on land now associated with the abbey. Perhaps Tewdric had organised his hermitage somewhere nearby; we do not know. Given Tintern's suitability as a fording place for the river Wye, we might wonder just how isolated and remote his hermitage was amongst the celebrated 'rocks' of the Book of Llandaff in any case. Perhaps he dwelt comfortably enough in a little settlement with a few chosen followers who could keep an eye on him in his old age. Again, we do not know.

The Wye is fordable at Tintern at low tide, though few might care nowadays to flounder through the mud. There is no reason why some sort of causeway should not formerly have overcome this, of course. Many battles were fought at fords, and Tewdric's was in that tradition. A tidal ford such as this was also a boon to cattle lifters, crossing at low tide on a moonlit night and counting on the rising river to impede any later hue and cry in pursuit of them. It was accordingly important for rulers to know who was crossing into or out of their territory, and why they were travelling. Such intelligence was equally necessary to the Kings of Morgannwg and the later Norman Lords of Striguil (*Y Strigwl* – 'a bend', in the river; *Striguil* in the Domesday Book. Chepstow is English – 'Cheap Stowe', a place where merchants gather / a market place, cf Cheapside in London). The Tintern area is easily reached by quite substantial boats, too, and before engineered roads, railways, and powered transport became the normal means of travel, the Wye was a well used route for goods and people making their way to and from destinations as far inland as Hereford. There were also taxes /duties to be collected on certain types of goods in transit, and fishing rights to be guarded jealously. In short, the area was of interest to any government. We should read the Book of Llandaff with such matters in mind.

Possibly the politics underlying the tone of the Book of Llandaff may be taken a little further. Tewdric's last wish is recorded as having been to be buried on what is generally taken to be Flat Holm island in the Severn Sea. This is at variance with the tradition recorded upon his memorial in Mathern church, however, which states;- "Here lyeth intombed the body of Theodorick, King of Morgannuck or Glamorgan, commonly called St Thewdrick and accounted a martyr because he was slain in battle against Saxons, being then pagans, and in defence of the Christian religion. The battle was fought at Tintern, where he obtained a great victory. He died here on his way homeward three days after the battle, having taken order with Maurice, his son, who succeeded him in his kingdom, that in the same place he should happen to to decease a Church should be built and his body buried in ye same: which was accordingly performed in the year 600."

This memorial dates from around 1610, however, and owes its existence to Bishop Francis Godwin of Llandaff, who at about this time wrote from Mathern to a friend in London;- "The manor of Mathern where there is now a palace, was given to the bishops of Llandaff by Maurice, King of Glamorganshire, about the year 650, on the following occasion: His father, St, Theoderic, as he is usually called, having resigned his crown to his son, embraced the life of a hermit. The Saxons invading the country, Theoderic was reluctantly called from his hermitage to take command of the army; he defeated them near Tintern on the Wye; being mortally wounded in the engagement he precipitated his return that he might die among his friends, and desired his son to erect a church and bury him where he breathed his last; he had scarcely proceeded five miles, when he expired at a place near the conflux of the Wye and the Severn; hence, according to his desire, a small chapel being erected, his body was place in a stone coffin. As I was giving orders to repair this coffin, which was either broken by chance or decayed by age, I discovered his bones, not in the smallest degree changed, though after a period of 1,000 years, the skull retaining the aperture of a large wound, which appeared as if it had been recently inflicted.

"Maurice gave the contiguous estate to the church, and assigned to the place the name Merthyr Tewdrick, or the martyrdom of St Theoderic, who, because he perished in battle against the enemies of the Christian name, is esteemed a martyr." (*Quoted from Coxe's 'Monmouthsire'*)

As we can see, Bishop Godwin's version of Tewdric's last wishes differs from the Book of Llandaff's. Certainly Bishop Godwin had seen The Book, "Saint Taylor's Book" (*Sic*, St Teilo's) he calls it in his letter, and adds that he will bring it with him when next he comes to London. We do not know if it ever made that journey. The difference may lie in the Bishop's memory, or with a version of Tewdric's tale being particularly well known in outline in the Mathern area, and quoted by him without thinking. We would expect local interest in it to be aroused by the discovery of bones which match the circumstances of Tewdric's death, which is all we can truthfully claim, so presumably plenty of people were talking about their saint at the time he wrote. Familiarity could have brought with it carelessness accordingly.

This was the case in about 1880 when St Tewdric's church was 'restored' in the Victorian fashion of those times. Mercifully only a little 'heritage' damage was done in the process, but Tewdric's supposed grave was rediscovered. A young lady of about 12 years old happened to visit the church while the grave was open, and was shown the bones by the then Vicar. She recalled, in 1946, that they were of a big, hefty man, and that the skull had a clean-cut wound in it. These things she told to Fred Hando, a journalist who at the time toured Monmouthshire and wrote of churches and other ancient sites. Being a useful pen-and-ink artist, he also drew his own illustrations to complement his articles. Yet by the time this present author settled in Mathern in 1970, the lady's name was forgotten, her family could not be traced, and no knowledge of the tomb's exact location existed. This is the current position.

A word of explanation about Mathern Palace, mentioned in Bishop Godwin's letter, is in order. The palace dates from around 1280 and in 1333 "Bishop John of Eglescliffe" was in residence there when he granted an indulgence of forty days to all who would contribute to the repair of a chapel . . . in the diocese of Lincoln! This is our earliest dated and specific reference to the palace. It was the official residence in Wales for the Bishops of Llandaff, and is situated on the old eastern shoreline of the tidal inlet of St. Pierre Pill, a very ancient haven for boats plying to and from the English side of the Severn estuary. For the Bishops this had the advantage of allowing them to be carried by boat right into their own back garden, which convenience could serve equally as a quick escape route to Bristol in times of political unrest. The Palace was much modified over the years, and in its present form is privately owned, the old landing stage remaining as one side of the Bishops' fish ponds in its grounds. The connection with the Pill is nowadays a mere ditch, along which flows water from both the fish ponds and St. Tewdric's well. We have a deal to tell about the latter later.

To add an interesting side-light to Bishop Godwin's claims to fame – he was later 'translated' to the See of Hereford – he had a well-informed and lively imagination, and was the author of a little work of early science-fiction entitled 'The Man in the Moone'. For his hero he created the person of 'Speedy' Gonzalez, an intrepid, pioneer, goose-propelled, Copernican lunarnaut. His book is still in print and is a fascinating read, – whole heartedly recommended.

But back to the Book of Llandaff; Tewdric's wish to be buried on Flat Holm may echo its use as an island retreat by saints of the Celtic tradition. One such was St Gildas the Wise, of whom we shall speak again, a priest of immense learning and terrific, bad-tempered, polemical outbursts against such ills of the age as those in which he himself was not implicated. His frustration with his time's declining Latin culture and political practice blasts through his surviving works. No doubt he gave his contemporaries some cause for embarrass-ment, and himself those medical ills associated with hypertension. But by default he was a (bad) historian, dropping hints when clearly he could have given details, as though implying that those amongst his readers who could not follow his writings were too ignorant and generally dim-witted to be worth his attention or company. Many in this category, of course, may well have played up to his estimation of them, and so have led cheerier lives in his absence. To calm down a little, perhaps, he himself had once gone to Flat Holm to meditate and study in the peace and quiet the island's isolation offered him. But 'Murphy's Law' intervened in the form of a boatload of Irish pirates. He ended up hiding from them in an uncomfortable little cleft in the rocks. One has to feel a pang or two of sympathy for him. Yet is the Book of Llandaff consciously implying that, in recording the use of Flat Holm by famous clerics, it is confirming a strong and ancient Christian tradition originating long before the Continental inroads of Normans, Cistercians, and the Papal monetary exactions of the Roman Catholic Church itself? Who can say? We must simply be a little cautious as we read from it, and pursue our own investigations of the era.

So how do Tewdric and his battle at Tintern fit into the scope of events in the wider world? We can no longer avoid names, dates and overall structure.

2

The Times of Tewdric – Britannia Slides into 'The Dark Ages'

Tewdric and Meurig are not Welsh names, although, in honour of his reign perhaps, Meurig has since become one. They are in origin of Gothic/Greek extraction. Why, out of the blue and unprecedented, were they chosen in the 6th century by a Welsh dynasty?

Here we have to recall that we are peering at what can be discerned of Roman Britannia following the collapse of the forms and traditions of almost 400 years of Roman rule. The Roman Empire had arrived, undesired and unwelcome, with the Claudian invasion of AD 43, and departed in 410 after the Goths from beyond its mid-European frontiers had marched into Gaul across the frozen Rhine in the winter of 406/7. In two bands, Visigoths and Ostrogoths, they swept through Italy, North Africa, and Spain. In 410 the Ostrogoths laid siege to Rome, sacked it, and established themselves as the 'de facto' rulers of the Western half of the Empire. In Britannia these events must have looked like the shameful end of the world to all Romanised Britons who identified strongly with the Empire, now conquered by 'barbarians'. The immediate practical impact of the change was to make communication between Rome and Britain very difficult, for affairs both of State and the newly organised Church, and the Britons were told to look after themselves as best they could. This much is clear and undeniable. It shapes all the history that follows, right down to our own day.

Britannia from a Roman point of view was a distant province on the very edge of the Ocean Stream (Atlantic) encircling a flat Earth which only a few fidgety, over-clever Greeks insisted was a globe. For practical purposes, and the Romans were very practical as opposed to speculative, such things did not matter. Britannia – that is, England and Wales – was conquered by the military skill of Aulus Plautius serving the Emperor Claudius, who contrived to arrive on the scene in time (AD 43) to accept the surrender of the Trinovantes' kingdom at Camulodunum (present day Colchester). Claudius could thus appear to have achieved more than Julius Caesar. This gave him, as a scholarly, elderly and unwarlike Emperor, the necessary military gloss to support his rule, and also added some extra property to the Empire. Was this really to Rome's benefit?

There was little gold to be had, but it yielded useful amounts of lead, tin, copper, grain, superior hunting dogs, and occasional supplies of slaves – if there had been some border warfare with the Picts (in Caledonia/Scotland). Although it took the Romans roughly a further 20 years campaigning to bring all Britannia under their effective control, at least local warfare amongst the indigenous tribal kingdoms was ended. A network of military roads was established, and these eased the movement of goods, people, and livestock under the *Pax Romana* to the markets of the newly formed 'civilising' towns, a particular feature of the Roman presence in the land. Equally, defence and peace-keeping in Britannia tied down as many as three legions, as well as the *limitanei* troops manning Hadrian's Wall, with other contingents assigned to the North Sea fleet (*classis Britannica*) and the Forts of the Saxon Shore, all at a considerable cost to the Empire. Whilst this military presence fluctuated much over the centuries, Britannia never became a tremendously profitable asset to Rome, to be held at all costs.

This was Britannia's status throughout some 400 years, a dozen or so generations. A Briton who was prepared to be assimilated into its Romanised culture and ways was able to prosper, play a substantial part in his local government, travel with much the same degree of safety as is enjoyed nowadays, and lead a life which allowed him to fulfil a good many of his ambitions. He may well have become literate, found wisdom in the writings of others, developed practical skills unknown to his more settled and rustic forebears, and married advantageously into the ranks of the ruling conquerors. Many of his fellow citizens would not have achieved as much, of course, nor even particularly have wished to. There remained a division between the 'Romanitas' sections of society, and the 'Brituncuii' – "the little Brits" – written of with an implied sneer, it seems, in one of the surviving notes scribbled for day-to-day purposes by the garrison of Vindolanda on Hadrian's Wall. No doubt the (simply appalling!) Brituncuii were well aware of this snobbish view of them, and some sought to adopt Roman names to indicate their allegiance to the Empire. In this way Theoderic, imperfectly pronounced, became Tewdric, Maurice – Meurig, Tacitus – Tegid, Constantine – Custennin, Paternus – Padarn, Maximus – Macsen, Patricius – Patrick, Ambrosius – Emrys, and many more, likewise. They told of one's status of choice, it seems, just as today many Hong-Kong and Taiwan Chinese adopt 'Western' names implying, perhaps, that although of the mainland Chinese race and civilisation, they embrace a certain special personal outlook, with all the acquired political and cultural assumptions that this implies. The same, it seems, applied in Britannia; 'Get Romanised, get on, and get rich . . .', perhaps.

In summary this looks pretty rosy and cosy, but probably life in Britannia was not all 'Latin lingo' (*lingua Latina*) and sunshine. There was a noticeable tendency for the legions in Britannia to support the ambitions of such of their commanders who sought from time to time to become Roman Emperors. This trait, if such it was, underlines the great fundamental weakness of Roman Imperial politics; no system was ever developed which permitted the smooth, legal, peaceful transfer of imperial power from each Emperor to his successor.

This problem had its origin in the time of the Roman Republic, which had effectively ended at the Adriatic sea battle off Actium in 31 BC, when the combined Roman – Egyptian fleets of Marc Antony and Cleopatra were demolished by Octavian/Augustus, the first Emperor. Under the old Republican system all who sought a career in public life at national level, the jealously guarded privilege of Senatorial families, made their way to prominence of some description via the *Cursus Honorum.* This was a hands-on training system by which young men, never women, undertook administrative/political jobs of real and increasing responsibility in both civil and military roles from their late teens onwards. Its great strength lay in giving future rulers a 'sharp-end' taste of real authority with its accompanying responsibilities in their contemporary world.

In this way no self-regarding, quasi-ideological, political theorists and bigots from cradle onwards emerged to take charge of everything and imagine themselves superior beings. All upon the *Cursus Honorum* had had to show themselves capable in public affairs, or remain in private life. Their allies, rivals, and enemies alike had all had a chance to evaluate their strengths and weaknesses, and themselves manoeuvre around them accordingly in their own careers. In time, under the increased needs of Empire, the *Cursus* was opened to the 'Knights' (*Equites*) who ranked below the Senators, but whose persons and families could be 'promoted' to wear the purple Senatorial stripe upon their togas if they were sufficiently able, effective, and ruthless in the Empire's interests. A widely-known Knight is Pontius Pilate of the Gospels, as also were his successors Felix and Festus (Acts of the Apostles).

However, with all power ultimately depending upon the Emperor and a limited body of possible successors to him if the office were not to become hereditary, it soon became clear to all ambitious Romans that the ultimate authority in the Empire resided in the brute force of the legions. As early as AD 68/69 came the Year of the Four Emperors, three of whom slugged it out with such forces as they had, regardless of a continuing four years' old full-scale insurrection in Palestine. Finally 'Daddy' Vespasian left his nasty little son Titus in command of operations to crush the Jews, and came to Rome from the Jerusalem front. On arrival he casually mentioned that he had large reserves available in the Balkans which were far nearer Rome than besieged Jerusalem, and, come to that, he could prevent the sailing of the Egyptian grain transports which kept Rome fed. Wonder of wonders, he instantly became Emperor with barely noticeable bloodshed to back his words, and died peacefully in bed ten years later, quite a 'good' Emperor as Emperors went. The shock to Roman society of the events of AD 68/69 concentrated minds powerfully, and there emerged over time a little clique of families and interests which looked to military solutions, manoeuvred, threatened, or battled out, to settle Imperial successions. From the end of the second century onwards these sapped the Empire's manpower, political stability, credibility, and overall morale, and the military activities of ambitious men became more important than the general welfare. The rot had set in. Essentially Rome's Empire ended in the West by a slow suicide of a thousand cuts.

All this politicking in Rome could not occur without having some effect even in far-off Britannia, which possibly suffered from it the more for not having been completely conquered. Rome knew that mainland Britannia was an island; a mutinous naval crew had sailed right around it in the time of the Emperor Tiberius (14-37) and a proper naval expedition confirmed the fact during the reign of the Emperor Domitian (81–96). Later, attempts were made to subdue the Picts, but the entire 9th Legion disappeared in one of them, and was hastily reconstituted by secondments from other legions in order to falsify the records of an obvious disaster. This, at least, is the romantic conjecture. Quite possibly the Picts were simply shrugged off by Rome, and the 9th transferred to some rather uninteresting and thus little-mentioned part of the Empire.

The Antonine Wall, stretching from the Clyde to the Firth of Forth, was a mid second century vainglory project of the Emperor whose name it bears, and was abandoned after a decent interval. The Picts remained a disruptive aggravation of thieves and pillagers seizing their chances, but never had their lands permanently laid waste by Rome as had happened elsewhere in the Empire. So they were always there for a would-be Emperor lacking a prestigious military victory to 'bash' a little, at no great cost, and as a possible training exercise for the *limitanei* garrison of Hadrian's Wall. Thus a capable and ambitious soldier could 'subdue' the Picts, or 'rescue' Britannia from them, a very long way away from the clique in Rome, to whose morning receptions he could return with a glowing account of his prowess in the field. All such additions to his reputation contributed great substance to his CV, assuming, that is, that news of anything untoward had not also reached the clique's influential ears. Such military self-glorifying appears to have become something of a system in the *Cursus Honorum*.

The Emperor Diocletian (284-305) was fully aware of the basic 'succession flaw' in the Imperial structure. He could scarcely have been otherwise, there having been seventeen Emperors between the murder of Severus Alexander in 235 and the accession of Valerian in 253; almost one a year! Diocletian tried to correct matters by formally dividing the Empire, with a separate Emperor at Byzantium (Constantinople) to rule in the East, whilst another Emperor in Rome looked after the Empire's Western affairs. To assist each there was a Sub-Emperor known as a *Caesar,* who was in a position to rise to the Imperial office and appoint his own *Caesar* when the ruling Emperor, East or West, retired or died, – and so on. To set a good example, Diocletian himself retired, and lived a further eight years. With hindsight, or to a contemporary politically astute cynic, his system never stood a chance.

Even as Diocletian wrestled with The Succession Problem, the 'Western' Roman Emperor, Maximian, became concerned about raids upon Britannia by 'Saxons' sailing over the sea from lands to the north of Roman Gaul. Therefore, to 'save' Britannia in his own name he appointed a naval officer from Belgium to conduct operations against them with an enhanced fleet from Rome's base at Boulogne. This man's name was –

Carausius; 287-293 After defeating and despoiling these troublesome seaborne raiders off Britannia's south coast, Carausius somehow forgot to return their loot to its British owners. Instead, he declared himself Emperor of Britain and North Gaul. Rome was obliged to recognise him for a few years, and then arranged for his assassination by one Allectus, who tried to become Emperor in his stead. He was rejected by the Britannic administration, and murdered in his turn. The official history states that Rome then rescued Britannia from the hordes of Picts and Scots who had taken advantage of the political confusion in the island. More likely this 'rescuer', Constantine Chlorus, by then the Western Emperor in Diocletian's scheme of things, simply came and did a little Pict Bashing somewhere in the north country, or even beyond Hadrian's Wall. This much achieved, and covered in all the glory attending a victorious military 'rescue campaign', he struck a medal to commemorate and publicise it, and wrote his own report of the business to consolidate his position. He died at the Roman field army headquarters in York before making any more moves he might have had in mind.

By his attempt at becoming Emperor Carausius had set his successors in high command in Britannia a bad example, if one were needed. Every time one of them went to try his luck on the Continent he naturally took his best troops with him, promising them glory, plunder, and a soft life as the new Praetorian Guard in Rome if they all succeeded in getting that far and remaining there. Whilst the legions in Britannia were patched up after each such event, the quality of the troops sent to such a benighted outpost was bound to be less than the elite, and it is doubtful that legions were even maintained at anywhere near full strength. Over time their ability to protect the island diminished and, whilst certainly no token force, after each attempted usurpation their usefulness seems to have declined a little further. By the late fourth century they were just a Roman remnant, their numbers much swelled by semi-Romanised recruits from around the Empire and auxiliaries who most likely served for their pay and lacked interest in the grand Imperial Ideal. The decline in military effectiveness had well and truly set in as each ambitious rebelling commander extracted more of the best from what was available to him. The following events highlight its progress.

Constantine-the-Great 306-337 He was acclaimed as a Sub-Emperor by the legionaries at York. He took the best troops among them to the Continent, collected support form the legions in Gaul, defeated his political rival at the Milvian Bridge within sight of Rome (312), became a Christian as the direct result of this victory, recognised Christianity as a 'legal' religion within the Empire (Edict of Milan 313), made his capital at Byzantium (330), renamed it Constantinople, and died (337). He does not seem to have have done anything political or military in Britannia's favour, but could claim the perfect example of a glittering official Roman career.

Constans 337-350 Youngest son of Constantine the Great. As Emperor he made a winter visit to wild and distant Britannia in 343, an undertaking which was considered very dangerous and daring. A winter

Channel crossing could be made to appear tantamount to space travel, back in far-away Rome. He may have 'bashed' a Pict or two, but we do not know; we only have a chance reference to the winter Channel crossing presented as a flattering addition to his prestige. No doubt those actually governing in Britannia had their own views about him.

The 'Barbarica Conspirata' 367 This year the 'barbarian' Picts, Scots (Irish), and 'Saxons' all raided Britannia in force. Then, and subsequently, it was suggested that there was a degree of collusion in their activity, a conspiracy for allied and concerted action. From such accounts as we have, there is a consistent tale of great damage done to Britannia's peace and quiet. Nor do the Empire's forces seem to have acquitted themselves with the customary degree of triumphant glory. Fullofaudes their C-in-C *(Dux Britannorum)* was captured, and Nectaridus, O-i-C of the Eastern defences, the Count of the Saxon Shore *(Comes Litorae Saxoni)* was killed. These events are taken to represent the overwhelming degree of the disaster. Equally, the two separate incidents may have been simple bad luck in furious and vicious fighting at close quarters. Nonetheless, it would seem that for a while hostile bands roamed Britannia and did much as they pleased. To aid the reassertion of its authority Rome sent Count Theodosius, a fairly junior officer, whose forces helped drive out the intruders, strengthened fortifications and, interestingly, proclaimed an amnesty for all Roman troops who had deserted their posts or otherwise failed in their duty. There is a suspicion that, due to corruption, their proper rations had not been supplied to them, and that discontent had led to passive obstruction if not outright mutiny. Obviously this would have been played down in official reporting, and we ought also to note that Count Theodosius was the father of a future Eastern Emperor (Theodosius I 379-395) who was ruling at the time that our main source, army veteran Ammianus Marcellinus, was writing his histories (*the 'Gestae'*) in Rome during the years 392-400. Care and tact in constructing the narrative were in order, therefore. Our voluble acquaintance St Gildas assures us that the lessons of the Barbarica Conspirata were "... soon forgotten ..." So just how frightful had the episode actually been, overall? We shall return to this later.

Magnus Maximus 383-388 Originally of Spanish origin Maximus was possibly the *Dux Britannorum* of the time. After carefully securing his rear by flattering and bolstering the indigenous auxiliary forces of Britannia, he took the pick of the Roman troops to the Continent, slew the Western Emperor Gratian, and ruled in his stead until being duly eliminated by Theodosius I in 388. The (simple!) Britunculi had taken him very much to their hearts as Macsen Wledig (*Prince/Chieftain Macsen*), and perhaps thought that 'one of their own' would surely eradicate the clique and give good Imperial government based on decency and common sense, such as these qualities were perceived in far-off Britannia. If so the idea was very parochial, and has often in such circumstances deluded peoples and nations since.

Niall-of-the-Nine-Hostages c395 Niall was the largely nominal High King of Ireland. At about this time he led two piratical raids, one upon Chester, the other on Caerleon. Technically these centres had been Roman legionary bases. What Niall raided were probably nearer to the condition of the late 1940s post-war aerodromes of East Anglia where squatters sheltered following RAF and USAF withdrawal, and where a variety of people, some of them entirely respectable farmers who had been dispossessed of this land "… for the duration of the war …" came and carried away all that was left behind which was useful to them and portable. The lack of 'Roman' ability to safeguard this property is nonetheless noteworthy, and often subject to many extravagant interpretations.

Constantine III 407-c411 This Constantine, with one Geraint as his lieutenant, developed Imperial ambitions and took whatever military force was available to him to the Continent, where by 411 they had all perished in the general military turmoil of invading Avars, Goths, and Franks, pushed forward from the rear by Attila and his Huns.

The Rescript of Honorius 410 The British, as we should now call them, towns had contacted Rome to state that although they were still loyal to the Empire and 'Romanitas' governance they had decided to look to their own defences. Probably they were simply stating that their duty to report the outcome of local elections to Rome had been interrupted by the collapse of the postal service following 'barbarian' inroads into Roman Gaul, so they were going to carry on as normal and send the documentation once able to do so. Emperor Honorius replied that they had better organise the security of their own "... towns and cantonments ..." for the indefinite future. Just possibly the bureaucrat drafting the Rescript thought he was addressing somewhere in Brittany where the barbarian problem was then particularly acute; an historically insecure but interesting comment upon the times.

Vortigern c 425-c461 Britain was now separated from the Western Roman Empire, whilst this still staggered on. It seems that the established way of life continued much as usual, including occasional raids by Picts and Scots. Our tradition, backed by such accounts as that of St Gildas (c500-c570) to whom reference is made only because he was in a position to know and certainly not because he possessed any capacity as a conscientious historian, is of a nation of peaceable, passive and utterly pathetic souls being plundered and massacred daily by devilish brutes. If the canons of that petty, smug, and self-restrictive mind-set known as 'Political Correctness' had been in existence at this time, the British would have provided a classic stock of feckless PC 'victims'. And it follows, according to this sham morality and pretended concern, that 'victims' must necessarily have excessively cruel 'victimisers'. Any non-Briton at this time will fill that role to perfection for PC purposes as advanced by St Gildas.

Sometime around 446 the British sent a letter to one Aetius, the Commander of forces in Gaul still fighting for the Imperial interest. Quoted word for word from St. Gildas' account by The Venerable St Bede (c673-735) it begins, "To Aetius, thrice consul, come the groans of the Britons ..." and complains "... The barbarians drive us into the sea, and the sea drives us back to the barbarians. Between these, two deadly alternatives confront us; drowning or slaughter ..." Aetius did not respond. He had his hands full with the Huns whom he defeated but did not eliminate, lest the results of a larger battle should reduce his own forces to the extent that they would be at the mercy of the

Visigoths, who were his allies against the Huns but would happily turn upon him once the Hun threat had ceased. In making this decision his judgement was sound, and the sudden death in 453 of Attila, the Huns' leader, gave Gaul a needed breathing space before, almost in their turn, the Franks made their move to conquer it. But Britain was on its own.

Our tradition has it that the Picts, Scots, and 'Saxons' were rampaging all over the land once more. These 'Saxons' could have been Saxons, Angles, Jutes, Franks, Batavians, Frisians, Rhenish/Ripuarian Franks and any other non Latin-speaking element congenial to the narrator, and embarking between Boulogne and Bergen. We shall refer to them as 'English', for collective purposes at least. Ravaging English had traditionally been put down by a Roman rescuer, and from the fog and shadows steps the problematic figure of Vortigern. In some traditions he is Macsen Wledig's British son-in-law, which should make us wary of anything else super-heroic spoken of him. His name itself can mean something like 'Great Leader' or 'Boss Man', but is it a name or a title? We cannot know. He may have been based in what is now Kent, but this again is uncertain. Vortigern suitably subdued the current insurgents, and then in about 450 invited 'Saxon' mercenaries from the Continent to come and enlarge the forces at his command. He settled them on British lands (as the Romans would have done) and all was well until they saw that they could be a power in their own right and revolted in an attempted war of conquest. Such, at least, is the tradition handed down to us. Vortigern fled, disappeared from the records, and perhaps ended his life hiding in a little cove on the Lleyn peninsular, c461. Certainly there had been an upheaval, but it is all more legend than reliable reportage. We ought to be suspicious accordingly.

A Briton whose ancestors had '... worn the purple ...' ie had senatorial rank, according to St Gildas, now comes to centre stage circa 460. He restores order, drives out and/or resettles the mutinous 'Saxons', and is a Roman hero in the generally expected tradition. We know nothing reliable about him. His name was Ambrosius Aurelianus, or Emrys in Welsh. The Venerable Bede, again drawing on St. Gildas, describes him as "... a modest man of Roman origin, who was the sole survivor of the catastrophe (Vortigern's policies?) in which his royal (Sic) parents had perished. Under his leadership the Britons took up arms, challenged their conquerors to battle, and with God's help inflicted a defeat on them. Thenceforward victory swung first to one side, and then the other, until the battle of Mount Badon (*Mons Badonicus c490*) when the Britons made a considerable slaughter of the invaders.." Essentially he was an heroic British war lord, as was one Riothamus who is credited with commanding the implausibly large number of 12,000 troops, two legions' worth, and crossing the Channel in 469/70 to aid the Western Roman Emperor Anthemius (467-472) in a campaign in Gaul. They came to grief somewhere in the Loire Valley, however, but this military intervention and date are secure. So are we to believe that Britain had gone from being a land devastated and laid waste by every traditional enemy available prior to roughly 460, to a unified State able to recruit, equip, train, supply and convey to battle overseas in 469 two whole legions (*Sic!*) which, moreover, were not needed at home for defensive purposes? If so, the implication is that the land was at peace, not riven with dire violence and uncertainty. What is really happening here? Who was the enemy at Mount Badon, and where had its combatants come from; a local insurgency, or a foreign invasion?

Our tradition becomes even more magnificent. The customary enemies of Britain are swarming again by about 500, and along comes Arthur Pendragon, 'King' Arthur himself. Thousands of books have been written about him, some 2,000 or so of which are housed in a specialised library at Mold, Clwyd, some dozen miles west of Chester. To him is usually attributed the victory at Mount Badon, wherever that is. The hills around Bath look promising, but there are many other possibilities. This battle is always viewed as a key engagement, and can be dated with the usual degree of certainty to between c490 and 518. Arthur can be 'translated' as 'Bear Man' (cf 'Bear' Grylls, popular television outdoor man of our own times) and Pendragon/Head Dragon, perhaps a formal military title. Who knows?

The Byzantine historian Procopius writes of a significant number of English going back to Frisia, Saxonia, Jutland, and so on at about this time. As a defeated remnant, or did they only want a quiet life? Perhaps rumours of an easy living to be enjoyed in Britannia were not so true after all? An epidemic known to us as The Yellow Death swept through

Britain 547/49. This had the obvious impact upon society, and we think that all is quiet in the land until the 550s.

A chance remark of St. Gildas, picked up by the sharp eyes of Bede, suggests that the Britons and English formed, at about this time, two distinct parties sharing something of a common culture. Denouncing, as ever, the lives lived by his fellow Britons, St. Gildas adds, "... Among other unspeakable crimes ... they added this – that they never preached the Faith to the Saxons who dwelt among them." We shall follow up this rebuke.

However, Britain was slowly ceasing to be exclusively British from the 550s onwards. Embryonic English kingdoms are discernible. It is their squabblings and local wars that form the narrative of our early history henceforward, and Wales evolves from western Britannia. We wondered at the start of this chapter what the names Tewdric and Meurig were doing included in the Welsh genealogies. They were possibly a final fling at *Romanitas* by their dynasty. If we assume that a royal house would wish to identify with none inferior to ruling Emperors, they indicate fairly reliable dates for Tewdric and Meurig, too. Consider; – Western (Ostrogoth) Emperor Theoderic-the-Great ruling 493-526, and Eastern Emperor Maurice 582-602. If two royal babes of Morgannwg were to be honoured by sharing names with these Emperors, then Theoderic and Maurice were the rulers at the times of their births. And the babes grew up and retained a little *Romanitas* into their own times; maybe even into our own.

Let us now consider how far these traditional accounts of early Dark Age British history square with such evidence as there is about the time. Was it mostly a period of vain ambition, pillage and bloody conflict? For a start, how did the attackers of Britannia come to its shores?

3

Invaders, Raiders and Traders – Who Changed Britannia

Britannia, island in the Ocean Stream (Atlantic), far from Rome towards the edge of the world, only a short way by sea from Ultima Thula (probably the Faeroes or even Iceland), beyond which lay the Abyss. How brave were the Romans' leaders who embarked from Gaul and crossed the terrible Channel, even in the winter, in order to rescue Britannia from its enemies and internal disorders! This, as we have seen, was an acceptable view for the populace in Rome to be encouraged to hold. Let us continue with it a little; "... sailing was very hazardous in that vast, open sea, where the tides were high, and harbours almost non-existent. The Gauls' ships were built and rigged in a manner different from our own. They had much flatter bottoms to help them to ride shallow water caused by shoals and ebb tides. Exceptionally high bows and sterns fitted them for use in heavy seas and violent gales, and their hulls were made entirely of oak to enable them to withstand any amount of shocks and rough usage. Their cross-timbers, which consisted of beams a foot wide, were fastened with iron bolts as thick as a man's thumb. The anchors were secured with iron chains instead of ropes. They used sails made of raw hides or thin leather ... probably because they thought that ordinary (flax) sails would not stand the violent squalls of Ocean, and were not suitable for such heavy vessels ..." So to whom do we owe this information? St. Gildas in a calm mood, perhaps? An Imperial panegyrist? Not at all; our

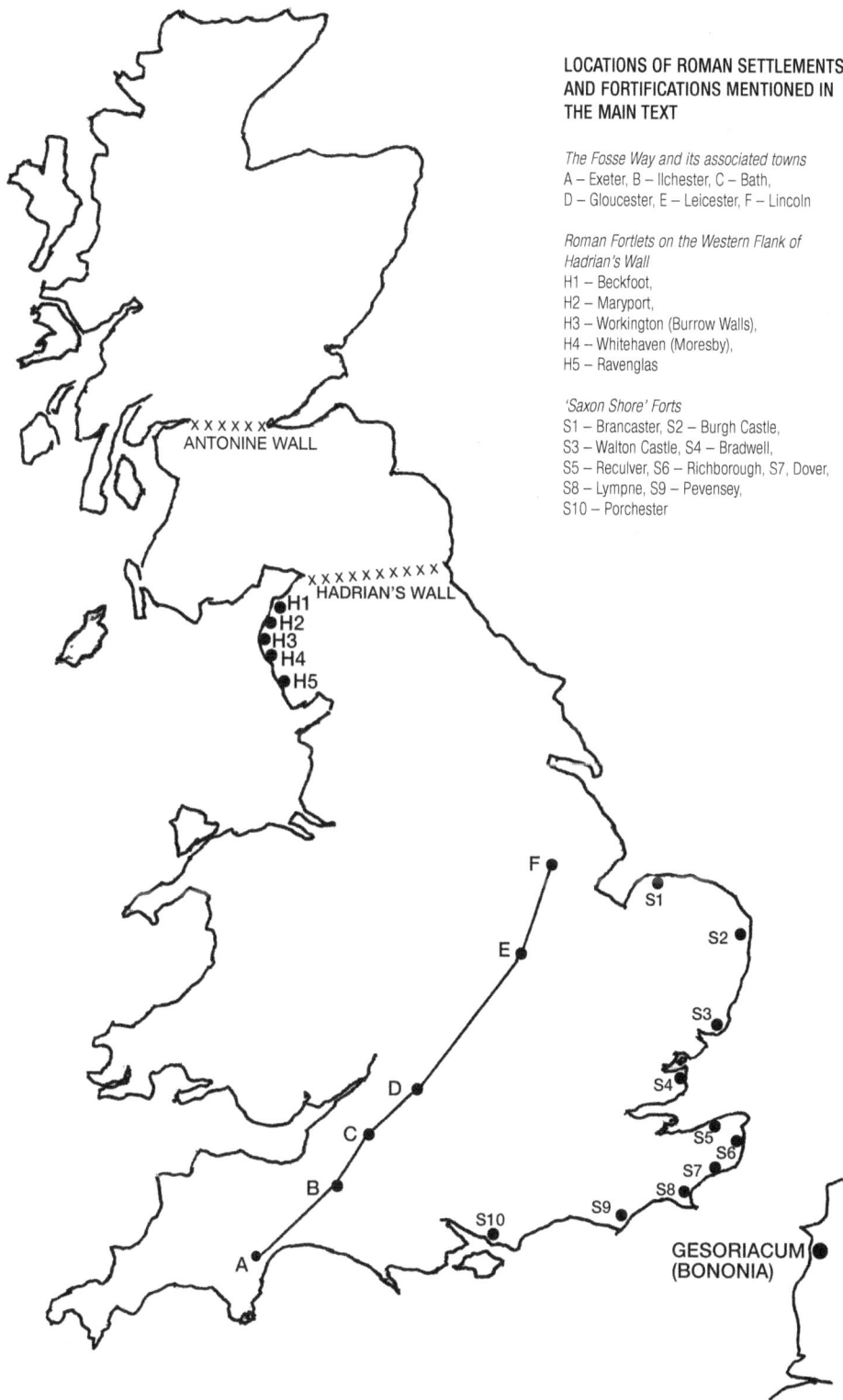

LOCATIONS OF ROMAN SETTLEMENTS
AND FORTIFICATIONS MENTIONED IN
THE MAIN TEXT

The Fosse Way and its associated towns
A – Exeter, B – Ilchester, C – Bath,
D – Gloucester, E – Leicester, F – Lincoln

*Roman Fortlets on the Western Flank of
Hadrian's Wall*
H1 – Beckfoot,
H2 – Maryport,
H3 – Workington (Burrow Walls),
H4 – Whitehaven (Moresby),
H5 – Ravenglas

'Saxon Shore' Forts
S1 – Brancaster, S2 – Burgh Castle,
S3 – Walton Castle, S4 – Bradwell,
S5 – Reculver, S6 – Richborough, S7, Dover,
S8 – Lympne, S9 – Pevensey,
S10 – Porchester

ANTONINE WALL

HADRIAN'S WALL

H1
H2
H3
H4
H5

F

E

S1

S2

S3

S4

S5
S6
S7
S8

D

C

B

S9

S10

A

GESORIACUM
(BONONIA)

informant is Julius Caesar, speaking of the Veneti (Bretons) with whom he was assiduously picking a fight in 56BC. In his usual way he writes his own report, 'violent squalls … heavy seas' and so on, implying outstanding bravery and achievement on the part of the all-conquering civilised Romans. But he also takes an intelligent interest in the people and technology he encounters.

In our dealing with "The Overthrow and Conquest of Britannia" (by the English), St. Gildas' own chosen title for his book on the subject, why should we look at Caesar's account of the way things were in coastal Brittany about 500 years earlier? Simply because Caesar is telling us that the (useless!) Britunculi certainly had knowledge of very seaworthy sailing boats, suitable for fishing and trading in the Atlantic and Western Approaches. It is conceivable that few of the Trinovantes and Iceni of East Anglia had seen such ships, but the British tribal kingdoms of the west – Dumnonii, Durotriges, Belgae – and in south Wales – Demetae and Silures – were well placed to be at least acquainted with their existence and their uses. To the people who depended upon them as a part of their normal way of life the sea was to be accorded all necessary respect with regard to the prevailing weather and tides, but it was certainly not to be viewed as barrier, a threat, or an elemental terror. This had likewise been the case for Phoenicians (of whatever lineage) in the Bronze Age, visiting Cornwall to trade for tin within the Doom Bar sand-bank at Padstow, amongst other places. They were comfortable when afloat and knew what they were doing upon great waters. We are looking at skilful seamen.

Likewise the Irish (Scots) and Picts had their curragh, a form of gig made from a lightweight frame of laths covered with leather/hides. It could carry half a dozen or more people, compatible with its size, and be rowed or sailed as the skipper chose. Its descendants are still in use on the Irish west coast for fishing, and the hides have yielded to tarred, tough canvas. A bracket for an outboard motor is likewise not unknown. Tradition apart, curraghs suit their owners' needs and the local conditions, just as the smaller, usually one-man, coracle bears salmon fishers with nets on shallow Welsh rivers. The curraghs could cross the Irish sea with ease. In 1975/'6/'7 one was sailed in easy stages – Faeroes, Iceland, Greenland – to America, and was chronicled in 'National Geographic Magazine' (December 1977). This experimental voyage gave substance to the archaeological evidence backing up a tradition of pre-Norse Irish hermits on Iceland, and the delightful tales about St Brendan the Navigator (c486-c575). To pick fact from fiction in his case is, frankly, a matter of personal choice. For example, did a demon rush down to the shore from a smoking mountain and throw firebrands at him, or did he see, or had a report of, an Icelandic volcano? It must be true, though, that a whale which rose from the deep to investigate the form of his curragh as seen from below, politely introduced itself as "Jasconius" before sounding again. Undeniably it spouted and drew breath – 'jas-con' – within the Saintly earshot.

Doubtless it was from curraghs that the Picts and Scots made their raids upon Britannia. Little bands simply sailed their craft around the ends of Hadrian's Wall, beached them in convenient places, hid them in the undergrowth, maybe even had arrangements with local (treacherous!) Britunculi to conceal them more securely in return for a share of the loot, stole – or borrowed on the same terms – some ponies, and went off to see what they could get. A long string of Roman fortlets on the Cumbrian coast testifies to the steps taken to curb these activities, once the would-be perpetrators were ashore. Bigger cavalry bases at Beckfoot, Maryport, Workington (Burrow Walls), Whitehaven (Moresby), and Ravenglass, tell of attempts to round up raiders who breached the first lines of defence or came more directly from Ireland. It must have been a matter of cat-and-mouse, successful and frustrating for both sides in about equal measure. By contrast the Antonine Wall is set with a string of forts, which may or may not have been effective. It was all quietly abandoned, later. One can almost hear an experienced local commander, wise from his own successes and failures in the area, muttering to himself, "So the Big Boss wants another wall, does he? Reckons he's solved all our problems, eh? Heigh-ho, we'll have to humour the fool. No help for that. A wall he wants, a wall he shall have. Let's hope there's enough budget left over to enrol a few more light cavalry. They'll do more good. And if we can get 'em, Big Boss will still claim the credit for his **** wall when they're successful. Such is life!" One can but sympathise.

The underlying point is that the sea, far from being a barrier to hostile bands looking for loot in Britannia, was a common and well used highway for them.

The same is true of East Anglia where the Forts of the Saxon shore rose up in the third and fourth centuries. They are now known as Brancaster, Burgh Castle, Walton Castle, Bradwell, Reculver, Richborough, Dover, Lympne, Pevensey, and Porchester. They were once credited to Count Theodosius sorting out the aftermath of the Barbarian Conspiracy, but archaeology has shown that their development occurred over time. Capable of exclusive military use, they are quite as likely to have served in addition as secure depots for official and civilian needs involving sea transport, the requirements for which must have altered much over the course of the centuries. Likewise some of the constructions termed shore 'signal stations' have a long and well-used history, whilst others among them were soon abandoned. All substantial buildings are capable of a variety of uses during their long lifetimes, which is true in these cases.

Raiders from across the Channel and the North Sea surely did not come in curragh-type boats to the exclusion of stouter shipping. Nor, come to that, do we need to confine the Picts, Scots, and Irish to these little vessels. As we have seen, the Veneti had good, robust, technically advanced, and very sea-worthy craft in the first century BC, and we can assume safely that the ones Caesar saw were but the latest examples of a type developed over a good stretch of time. The Romans had their own traditions of shipping both for warfare and trading, and these could also voyage under sail on the high seas from the Mediterranean to Britannia. In one form or another they had been doing this when trading, well before the Claudian conquest of AD 43. Rome had its Gallic port at Boulogne (*Bononia/Gesoriacum*), not too far from the marshy, island-studded mouths of the Rhine, and the natural tidal-lands of the Netherlands. Such terrain encourages boat-building, and breeds seamen. In short, well before AD 43 an expectation of sound, substantial, wooden boats making crossings of the North Sea and Channel under sail must be allowed. Admittedly our evidence for firm statements about these matters is scanty to non-existent, but a good old archaeological maxim runs, "Absence of evidence is not necessarily evidence of absence." The next season's digging may well provide the missing indications or objects to confirm a conjecture, or change the story altogether. Let us proceed from there.

From Nydam Mose (*mose = bog*) in southern Denmark we have a beautiful, double-ended, clinker-built, boat made of oak and dendro-dated to AD 310-320. It measures 23m long and 4m broad, and has provision for 30 rowers, plus a steersman with a steering oar on the starboard (*steer board*) stern quarter. It was deposited in the 'mose' as a 'ritual/sacrificial offering' at some time before about 450. That it should lack any apparent provision for a mast and sails is surprising, given its size, weight, and carrying capacity. A full-scale replica, adapted to sailing by the re-structuring of bow and stern, has behaved very well when tested at sea, in all essentials being a Viking 'dragon ship'. Tacitus (c55-c120) tells us that the northerly German boats had no sails; we do not know exactly what his informants saw, however. And for navigating tidal creeks, estuaries, and coastal waters the Nydam boat is an ideal craft. So to these we may confine its use, setting aside conjectures upon its having been a one-off State Barge for some important individual, or a 'ritual' vessel. For a certainty a craft of such sophistication did not spring spontaneously from the mind of a fourth century boat-builder. It is part of a tradition of skill and craftsman-ship of the highest order.

Across the sea, and right on The Saxon Shore at that, we have the 'ghost-ship' of Sutton Hoo near Woodbridge in Suffolk. We may forget The Flying Dutchman of legend and lore, but ghostliness is all we have of this magnificent 6th/7th century vessel. Its decayed imprint in the sand of Sutton Heath showed a phantom ship, and even this is now seen only in photographs, draughtsmen's plans and, even more palely, captured in plaster-of-Paris and a fibre-glass moulding. We owe its features to the competence and great care of Basil Brown, a self-taught 'digging' archaeologist and antiquary employed by Mrs Edith Pretty, JP, who owned the land upon which the 'howe' (*barrow, burial mound*) above the ship – as it turned out – was situated. In the summer of 1939 Basil Brown, joined later by a number of highly qualified archaeologists, painstakingly followed lines of stained sand visible in their trench. In a classic of brush and trowel excavation these minute shadings in the sand, and the tiny variations in its texture, led them to rows of rusty, rowelled, rivets which had once held together the overlapping planks of a majestic ship. After long weeks of stressful work helped by unusually dry weather, its full outline was visible. This was astonishing enough, but it proved to be the tomb of a Saxon King – probably Raedwald of the East Angles (died 624 or 625) – and such a portion of his personal treasure as was thought fit to dignify his royal remains in Eternity. Mrs Pretty presented the whole find to the Nation.

The ship measures 27m in length, 4.5m in width amidships, and drew 0.6m of water. Indications of its prow and stern were missing from the sand's imprint, but can be conjectured from the lie of the remains to have risen to something over 3.8m above the keel plank at its midship point. It was clinker-built with nine strakes a side, apparently open-decked, had 26 ribs stiffening its hull, and provision for 38 rowers for its propulsion. As with the Nydam boat, there are no obvious fixtures for a mast or sail. And this is equally perplexing in a ship which could have taken on anything normally expected of the North Sea quite comfort-ably. It is calculated that its rowers, plus steersman, could have propelled it at some four knots for all practical purposes. Thus a Channel crossing from Bononia/Gesoriacum (*Boulogne*) to Rutupiae (*Richborough*) would have taken its crew a tiring ten hours and upwards, even with wind and tides co-operating. A tubby Roman merchantman making perhaps six knots under sail on two masts could have, swan-like, contemptuously glided past its beautiful streamlined form, and disappeared in a couple of hours or so below the horizon which was beckoning to both crews. The significance of this would not have been lost on any seaman. The Sutton Hoo ship was probably built around 550. It was old and repaired – by evidence in the sand – and so expendable as a tomb vessel when interred in about 625. But 'Saxon' raiders and pirates were a problem for Britannia a good four hundred years earlier than this. With the Veneti vessels of 56 BC in mind, and the use of sail by Rome, something has to be wrong with our present appraisal and understanding of the nature of North Sea travel from at very least the third century onwards, be we never so careful with inter-preting the rather limited evidence available.

At the time of writing (October, 2018) a full scale replica of the Sutton Hoo ship is under construction in a boatyard by the river Deben at Woodbridge. Its building will be as authentically accurate as possible, using tools available in the sixth century and applying other features suitable for experimental archaeology. It will most probably be ready to launch in the late summer of 2019, *ceteris paribus,* and will thereafter be subjected to every trial and test devisable in the interests of increasing our knowledge of Dark-Age shipping. Beyond doubt a mast and sail will be tried out at some stage, and this may yield unexpected results. Time will tell.

Meanwhile, let us conjecture – dangerous practice! – a little.

Between Caesar's last botched attempt at invasion in 54 BC, carefully presented by him as a confirmatory reconnaissance in strength, and the Claudian invasion by Aulus Plautius in AD 43, contacts between the British kingdoms and an increasingly Romanised Gaul increased. There had long been trading in tin, wine, and luxury goods, but the stability in Gaul brought about by the *Pax Romana*, strictly on Rome's own terms of course, gave merchants a little more confidence and variety of goods to trade across the Channel. Rome consolidated its base at Gesoriacum /Bononia (*Boulogne*) and when Plautius sailed he seems to have had Rutupiae (*Richborough*) or its general area in his sights. The point is much debated; and a possible second fleet may have headed for the Chichester area near where client-King (?) Cogidubnus had, or very soon built, his 100% Roman 'des res' villa at Fishbourne. Therefore there existed sizeable ships which could make such journeys in invasion fleet strength, and skippers and pilots enough to guide them, willingly or at sword-point. In 60/61 when Boudicca led her revolt, Decianus Catus, the Governor whose enforcement of Rome's taxation policy and barbaric treatment of the Iceni royal family had sparked off the trouble, was able to flee quickly to Gaul and look innocent whilst Suetonius Paullinus the Roman Commander-in-Chief, who was not a very nice man either, smashed the revolt and butchered all the (uppity!) Britunculi he could catch. Even the Emperor Nero was upset at his excess of gratuitous violence, and had him replaced. An unexceptional and reliable two-way level of Channel-crossing traffic is again implied. By 286 when Carausius made his bid for the Empire, the protection of a fair level of valuable trading in the supposedly pirate-ridden Narrow Seas was his initial plausible excuse. Over 243 years had by then passed since the late-middle-aged Claudius had crossed and re-crossed the Channel to claim his share of military glory, so necessary for an Emperor. Therefore the sea, ventured upon with due common sense, was clearly viewed locally by all parties as manageable and not a terrible barrier to be approached by heroes only – certainly not in old Claudius' case.

Exactly what was trafficked between Gaul and Britannia is a wonderful hunting ground for archaeologists and scholars, especially with regard to the quantities of goods carried. On his way to becoming Emperor through a suitably complicated series of murders, trickery, general dirty politics and, finally, acclamation by his troops, Julian the Apostate (ruled 361-363) had supplied his garrisons on the Rhine with grain from Britannia in 358/9. Upwards of 600 ships were employed in the process, we are told. And whilst we may regard this figure in the same light as Riothamus' 12,000 troops in c467, there must have been a large number of ships, crews for them, and a knowledge of where to go and how to get there readily available. We can speculate indefinitely on whether a single huge fleet sailed, or whether there was a shuttling to and fro, and also what route they took to /up the Rhine. There is little to guide us bar the fact that calculations suggest that a legion of circa 6,000 men, at full strength, required around 8 tonnes of grain and fodder to per day to keep it going. In barracks this would have entailed a feat of some organisation, and in the field a fast-changing logistical challenge. Add in the Channel as a factor, and a mention of this particular supply achievement in the histories is perfectly proper. But was some level of British grain export to these garrisons a normal event, and only increased to large proportions by Julian as a reserve to boost his troops' morale as seizure of the Imperial title, preceded by warfare, became a possibility? Who can say? We only know that an estimated 40,000 tonnes of 'dry fodder' crossed to the Rhine in this operation.

The calculation is based upon the calculated capacity – 50 tonnes –

of the Blackfriars Roman boat which was found incorporated into the filling for an ancient wharf in London. It had been employed in carrying ragstone from quarries in Kent into *Londinium* to rebuild the city, after Boudicca had burned its first Roman version. Old and patched, it seems the boat sank where it was found and was not judged worthy of salvage. Whilst used as evidence in the calculation of the Rhenish grain supply, in practice a variety of craft could have been employed/requisitioned. It serves nonetheless to give us an idea of what was possible using normal means of transport by the mid 4th century. It had also had a sail.

So did North Sea skippers rely on large fit crews to bend to their oars for hours on end, or did they let the winds do most of the work at less expense? If Tacitus was entirely right about an 'oars only' North German tradition, there is no reason why a good few North Germans should not have adapted to sail once they had seen the Roman ships with a mainmast and a foremast, the latter sloping somewhat towards the bow in most illustrations. This eased steering. The sails depicted are rectangular, and the mainmast bore the larger. In a steady wind somewhat astern of them they sailed well, too. Some Mediterranean grain transports weighed in at around 1,000 tonnes; on one of these, probably, St Paul was shipwrecked en route to Rome (*Acts of the Apostles, Chapters 27–28.2*). We do not know if any came into the Channel or Narrow Seas. However, we are informed that Aulus Plautius had some elephants and a Camel Corps in his army in AD 43. They certainly did not swim over to these shores.

Once the post-Boudiccan reconstruction of Britannia was underway and the Province was at peace, with life's normal activities once more undertaken by all citizens, what would be more natural than for a 'Saxon' or so to be taken on as crew on a Roman trader which, through injury, sickness or desertion, had found itself a few hands short upon the point of sailing from Boulogne? A fit adventurous young 'Saxon', viewed as a barbarian – ie not a customary Latin speaker – could have been able in some dog-Latin or Oude Vlammandsespreek to have made it plain that he was used to boats. Indeed the skipper in need, perhaps only a first or second-generation Roman himself, may have been impressed by seeing how this 'Saxon' had handled his part in docking whatever craft had brought him into harbour, and so have signed him on for a short voyage of a few days to Britannia; basic wages, his rations afloat, and a couple of sesterci to spend if the cargo sold well. From such beginnings much may have grown.

Let us speculate further.

4

History or Histrionics?

"The barbarians drive us into the sea, and the sea drives us back to the barbarians. Between these, two deadly alternatives confront us, drowning or slaughter." Eh? Was "... Aetius, thrice Consul ..." to whom this outpouring was addressed as a plea for help, really supposed to take these "... groans of the Britons ..." at face value in 446? Or do we have St Gildas showing off his acquired Latin with this a burst of would-be classical rhetoric? Unless official correspondence was always conducted in this style, the groans would surely have come from Aetius. We have looked briefly at what the sea could have offered by way of potential groan generation. How were things ashore?

It had been 63 years since the Spanish general Magnus Maximus, good old Macsen Wledig to his Welsh chums (and extended family both by bloodline or acquired by subsequent boasting) had taken what may be regarded as the last properly trained and equipped Roman field army from Britannia to ... do what? Bring some sort of order to the murderous Imperial politics which had by then affected the ability of the Empire to defend its provinces, especially in this case 'remote' Britannia, or merely to join in the bloodbath and perhaps become Emperor – for a while? Magnus achieved the latter, and was duly murdered in 388 almost as a matter of routine. And then, for Britannia ... what? We must ask an awkward question at this stage. For a 'Romanised' Briton serving as a regular soldier in 446, what was there about the Roman Empire and the Imperial system of government that was worth fighting for, especially if this meant leaving home and family to the mercy of pillaging and plundering raids by external foes? Would not any legionaries who may still have existed have been better employed within Britannia's shores? Certainly, but whom would they have served, and to what ends would their force have been directed?

Traditionally the historical perspective has been to view the Imperial forces as being akin to patrolling police in our own day; one could never find a legion when one wanted one. And if there was not more than a grain of truth in this view it could hardly have stood the test of time. But were the (groaning!) Britunculi utterly prostrate and helpless, driven all over the land and massacred in their hundreds on a weekly basis? Could, in fact, a field army in Britannia really have been required not so much to drive out rapacious barbarians from beyond its frontiers as to enhance the effective executive power of a local political faction, the *'Romanitas Party'* let us call it? Let us move on from the scraps of recorded and deduced political history currently to hand, and see what archaeology can tell us.

Since the 1970s/80s British archaeology has changed in many ways, mostly for the better. New scientific techniques both in exca-vation and, post-digging, in laboratories have opened up not just a few dated and dogmatic points of view, but whole new vistas to what can be achieved for a price in hard cash; which factor is another story, as ever. If there was continuous chaos, bloodshed and misery immediately the last Roman troop transport had cast off its moorings and proceeded Gaulwards – under sail beyond doubt – what evidence have we for it beyond a few often oblique, partisan, and much-copied written texts? Frankly, practically none; to date (2018) it must in fairness be added. Our ground is still uncertain/un-dug. Yet the average Briton, of whatever ancestry, seems to have known a pretty quiet and secure life overall.

Let us consider the following; the evidence yielded by cemeteries. However horrible the alleged slaughter, one might expect there to have been a few survivors who, although maimed by wounds, had lived on after the battles, died later, and were then decently interred. Surely the evidence of the battering and cutting would be upon their bones? True, but consider the figures;-

Late Roman period; c250 – c450; 4,977 burials excavated; 18 blade injuries to skeletons, = 0.36%
'Western' (broadly west of the Fosse Way); c450 – c700 854 burials: 2 Injuries: = 0.23%
Anglo-Saxon – exclusive cemeteries; c450 – c700 3,020 burials: 40 injuries: = 1.3%

(Figures from summaries quoted by James Gerrard in 'The Ruin of Roman Britain')

These figures, often obtained from cemeteries dug as 'rescue digs' ahead of building or road construction, and therefore following no particular pre-conceived evidence-searching agendas, hardly suggest a daily expectation of violence and routine brutality. They mostly come from east of the Fosse Way, the Roman road which was probably the 'wild-western' frontier to the Province for a period following Aulus Plautius' operations after the Emperor Claudius' invasion of AD 43. It runs, using present-day town names:- Exeter, Ilchester, Bath, Cirencester, Leicester, Lincoln, and to some extent defines 'lowland' eastern England from the 'upland' west and Wales. It is always arguable that after a battle it was not possible to carry away the dead, and that the slain were stripped of all that might be useful to the victors of the field, and then left to the disposal of wolves, foxes, wild boar, eagles, buzzards, and other opportunist feeders. If so, then we might not come upon their dismembered remains, ever, which would skew the picture. But would it skew it very much? There is plenty about the 450 – 700 era to re-examine in depth and redefine.

Archaeology also shows us that there was no sudden panic building of defences around villas, villages and individual farms following the withdrawal of the legions. In Gaul, with many serious barbarian incursions and armies accompanying migrant bands manoeuvring around the outnumbered Roman forces, there are many defended buildings – often burned to the ground several times – and numbers of sacked and abandoned villas and settlements. Nothing like it is seen within these shores. Indeed, settlements which are undoubtedly English are as bare of defensive works as those of their (oppressed!) Britunculi neighbours. Where large buildings/villas were abandoned, for whatever reason, their remains usually suggest that they stood till the roof timbers gave way, and then slowly decayed from there. And how is it that these savage English were living alongside good (civilised!) Britunculi, apparently in harmony and neighbourliness?

Indeed, archaeology appears to suggest that there were far more English living peacefully with their British neighbours at this period than our long-accepted ideas assume. Whether they had originated from discharged auxiliary troops who had served with the legions, were ex-legionaries in their own right, or were straight-forward immigrants, archaeology cannot tell us. But if they were following the habits and customs of the period and doing the same sorts of things as their British neighbours, especially if there was a fair degree of inter-marriage, how might we tell the two strands of Anglo-British apart from the remains of their homes and their middens? We should tread carefully accordingly.

Let us consider St Gildas a little more; he at least wrote down his presumably honest opinions of his times, which were c500 – c570. So far as we know he was born north of Hadrian's Wall somewhere on upper Clydeside. He possibly had married, and became a monk only after the death of his wife, having lived an everyday life somewhere south of The Wall. He certainly received a first class education, probably at the monastery founded by St Illtud at Llanilltud Fawr (Llantwit Major) in south Wales. St Illtud is thought to have been a disciple of St Germanus of Auxerre (St Garmon in early Welsh; died 446 or 447) so the young Gildas had access to a direct intellectual tradition of *Roman-itas* deriving from someone who had been trained as an advocate in Roman Law, and who had been for a while Governor of Romanised Brittany. It seems that St Germanus only became seriously involved in the Church when he was appointed Bishop of Auxerre in 418 on the death of that See's incumbent. He had twice visited Britannia, and had led the Britons to victory in the amazing 'Hallelujah! War' c429 which we shall consider elsewhere. In short, at the monastery there was clearly much 'St Germanus' type of wisdom available in manuscript texts dealing with practical subjects, philosophy, history, law, and the Roman world view for a very provincial, grieving, and upset Gildas to latch on to and use to assert his acquired Christian *Romanitas*. Gildas' theology likewise is 100% orthodox and accords perfectly with St

Germanus' teachings. So Gildas, a backwoods interloper into *Roman-itas* via the Church, knew of the laws, culture and customs of Rome, but perhaps had been snubbed and subjected to less well-informed *Romanitas* snobbishness in various ways before becoming a priested evangelical monk, thus firing him all the more to correct the ways of the world in which he then moved.

We may assume that few clerics of the day could match him in knowledge, both religious and secular, and his ardour in damning the sins of those whom he considered should know better was probably counter-productive in its immediate effect. We might even suggest he was exorcising something of an inferiority complex. Yet to what extent was he, and *Romanitas* citizens generally, maintaining the intellectual ideas of a culture which no longer existed for day-to-day practical purposes? By 450 was the *'Romanitas Party'* anything more than a self-regarding clique, a sort of Senior Common Room in a particularly ivory-towered university-like mental environment bemoaning that the 'Ubiquitous They' – as in "Why don't **'they' *do*** something about all the things that we don't like?" – failed to come and create their fantasy world for them?

Gildas' annoyance that the tyrants/usurpers ruling their little king-doms in the late fifth and sixth centuries had never preached the Gospel to the 'Saxons', may be just another sin he can almost gleefully attribute to them. Equally it may reflect an anachronistic *'Romanitas Party'* outlook by which the early English were viewed even in their third, fourth, or subsequent generations as foreigners, tolerated for their occasional usefulness as auxiliary fighting men, but certainly not as 'proper' Britons who ought not to bear arms because this was forbidden to civilians under Roman law. But what might Anglo-British civilians of whatever origin have been expected to do if Pictish raiders appeared on the scene? Might they not have seized weapons/hunting kit and looked to someone like Vortigern to be their leader, long-estab-lished early English and indigenous British – themselves of multiple origins – fighting together to defend their common interest in maintain-ing peace, law/custom, and order, imposed for themselves and by themselves? Let *all* enemies beware! Therefore could the *Romanitas Party* appeal to Aetius in 446 have been for an army to be used as much to curb an assertive Anglo-British faction, so comprised, as to subdue 'Saxons' perceived as revolting as a result of Vortigern's policies and seeking to conquer the Province? This may have been nearer the reality of the times.

Vortigern appears to have had some form of legitimate status as the leader of a 'Council of the Britons', for want of a better description, which still looked upon itself as the proper authority in Britannia. He seems to have been most influential 430-450, during which time his 'party' dealt with invasion/disorders, and established a degree of tranquillity and prosperity which even allowed Riothamus to take his 12,000 (*Sic!*) fully equipped troops to Gaul in c470 to help *Romanitas* in the form of the Emperor Anthemius' campaign there. So regardless of the true number of these more-or-less fighting men, they do not appear to have been viewed by the *Romanitas Party* as necessary for the protection of Britannia. If broadly true, this is significant.

It is very odd policy indeed if the country had been in tumult and slaughter only a short while before. St Germanus' biographer, writing in c480, calls Britannia 'prosperous'. Is this simply a customary statement that is to be made for Roman readers about a Roman province, or does it reflect a fair degree of truth? We should note that our written sources tell of yet more English armed activity a little after this time, allegedly involving Vortigern's imported 'Saxon' mercenaries. This culminated in Ambrosius Aurelianus, whose '. . . parents had worn the purple . . .' but had been killed in the mayhem, leading armed and Romanised Britons to massacre English at Mount Badon. Every one of our sources agrees, or copies hopefully, that this battle was of major significance in re-establishing a desired *status quo,* whatever that may have meant in practical terms to the majority of the victors. We can, unfortunately, only give it the approximate date of between c490 and 518, during which time there is opportunity for plenty of politics of which we are ignorant to have happened.

At Mount Badon it is possible that there was a newly-created *Romanitas* force, mustered initially from the retainers of the great aristocratic landowners who in 410 had 'inherited' the huge Imperial estates west of the Fosse Way. This localised *gendarmerie* would have numbered a dozen or so 'enforcers' upon each estate/'kingdom', whose function was to make sure that local obligations to the estate were honoured, taxes in kind paid to their chiefs/'kings' (it seems a monetary economy had fizzled out by c490), order kept amongst the tenants, and any incursions of external enemies dealt with, possibly in conjunction with similar forces from neighbouring estates and conscripted irregulars judged able to fight. At Badon their numbers could have been swelled, we may suggest, by units comprised of career soldiery who were members and connections of this aspirational aristocracy, purple-wearers or not, and who had been fighting on the Continent in support of branches of these families resident in Brittany.

They would have been hardened warriors, well trained in disciplined fighting tactics. Whilst not exactly a formal legion, their effectiveness would have exceeded the efforts of Britons, English, and mercenary 'Saxons' combining together to acquire land on the free-hold terms which had been applicable to discharged legionaries further east. A clash of two forces so composed could have had but one outcome. If something like this had settled the 'Land Question', with the Fosse Way as the rough dividing line between the two different systems which in practice had grown apart over several generations, it would certainly have been a decisive event. We shall consider land tenure shortly. Regrettably we do not know enough about the politics of the period to be more assured of what exactly was achieved at Mount Badon, and to whose advantage. Perhaps, though, we can dimly perceive Wales emerging.

This is also the time when Arthur became active. Were he and Ambrosius fighting upon the same side for exactly the same reasons? Why does St Gildas not name Arthur, beyond dropping a dubious hint about King Cuneglasus, ruling most of central Wales, having been pleased enough in his youth to have served as 'charioteer' (*Sic*) to a warrior called 'the Bear' – '*yr Arth*' in Welsh. There are greater political subtleties to these years than a simple 'virtuous' Britons versus 'ravaging' Saxons division.

Let us recall that in 410 the 'Rescript of Honorius' had told the rulers of Britannia to continue in ruling and defending themselves. The implication is that this is what they were in effect doing already. By the time of our earliest reckoning for Mount Badon c490 two or three generations have taken over the tasks of government in, effectively, national as opposed to provincial terms. Indeed, the full *Romanitas* procedures may have begun to run down with the departure of the 'last' legionaries with Magnus Maximus in 383. For a start, there were no more taxes going to Rome; certainly not after 410. So money/goods/crops collected locally for taxes, which might have been10% of the Gross Domestic Product of Britannia as calculated by some historians, were kept in the hands of the wealth-producers and may not have been handed in to a 'Council of the Britons' at all. Thus the country was to that additional extent 'prosperous', as St Germanus' biographer states.

Traditionally historians tell us that there was a massive economic collapse, as witnessed by the abandonment of a monetary economy, and depopulation of the crumbling run-down towns. Certainly archaeology agrees that towns were no longer important in the sense required by the ideology of 'civilising (uncouth!) Britunculi barbarians by urbanising them', which Rome imposed. But the same archaeology suggests that, whilst the built-up towns remained (to this day, indeed!) the (ungrateful!) Britunculi found plenty in them of which to make use. Was an ex-Roman council chamber (*curia*) any less effective against wind and weather as a cattle byre? With a bit of adaptation, would not a wall with tiled flues in it serve pretty well as the chimney for a forge? It was a pity to tramp all over the pretty mosaic floor in that room; or was it? Was a little revenge vandalism for former snobbishness quite sweet? But it was mighty agreeable for a smith to ply his trade in the dry. And if the town had some walls around it, it was fair enough to keep them in some sort of repair in case wandering plunderers came by. Or so thought the inhabitants of Cirencester, Colchester, Caerwent, Lincoln, York, London ... and many other places. They might not keep out an army but they served local needs at the time, and even inhibited stock from breaking loose and running off into the surrounding countryside on market days and fairs, when arranged. By and large ex-Britannia was getting along pretty well in its own preferred ways by 500.

So as the (ghastly!) Britunculi became – once again? – regional varieties of Briton over the 200 years or so which include the times we are now considering, who were they exactly? Our oldest (amazing!)

Britunculus could be the Mesolithic fellow who had lived in Gough's Cave, Cheddar, about 9,000 years ago, and whose direct descendant was discovered through a voluntary DNA survey of the area in 1997. His claim is not uncontested, however, and since the Mesolithic era a whole series of peoples have come to dwell within Britannia's shores. Taking the Fosse Way again to serve as a dividing line, lowland Britain to its east has seen more foreign settlers than are detectable further west. But there is a good genetic mixture of in-comers, and Caesar certainly found no single mitochondrial strand of (howling!) Britunculi DNA lining the cliffs to resist him. Once the legions had established themselves we may be sure that vigorous genetic material from all over the Roman world was added to the Britannic blend, one way and another, and the sea-faring early English from the Germanic/Norse lands certainly became a presence, possibly kept long identifiable by the *Romanitas* snobbishness of influential families.

At a purely practical level, though, it is perfectly possible that by about 250 a 'Roman' Siegmund and a 'Roman' (semi-Romanised Britunculus!) Gareth farmed alongside one another, as either free-holders or tenants of an estate. They bore (illegally, as Roman civilians) hunting spears and archery kit if Picts, Scots, Irish, brigands or 'unfriendly Saxons' turned up in their vicinity. They had an interest in common, namely their peace and quiet enjoyment of life, and they were prepared to defend it. Quite likely Vortigern was descended from such as they.

What lands might they have farmed? The biggest landowner in the Roman scheme of things had been The Emperor. The idea of land allocation, associated *in tandem* with the *cursus honorum,* was to establish a Romanised land-holding class of citizen throughout a standardised Empire. From this, good, loyal legionaries could be recruited for their 25 year term of service, and to it they could return on their discharge with their (compulsory) savings as a pension, and a freehold plot of Imperial land to farm. A splendid idea; in practice, though, Imperial lands were overseen by Roman stewards termed *Coloni,* who in this office over time became hereditary landowners in their own right, quite distancing themselves from the chopping and changing political courses of Imperial successions and attempted usurpations. To these fell the full title to such lands in 410, as we have noted. They had already been exercising *de facto* ownership, even to the extent of selling them or enlarging them by various means which do not matter here. The same system also was in place for all mines, and we know that only half the profits from these ever went to Rome. Therefore careful stewards of Imperial lands were immensely rich, by British standards, and were quite able to sub-let land on terms agreeable enough both to them and their tenants. Siegmund and Gareth, if the descendants of lease-holders under these arrangements, would have been living quite well by Tewdric's day. If their forebears had served in some section of the Roman army they would, of course, have been freeholders of inherited land, and on these terms there would have been plenty of Siegmunds among them, too.

The oft-mentioned *Numerus Hnaudifridi* (Notfried's Troop) were part of the garrison on Hadrian's Wall at some stage in its history. They had possibly come to Britannia as 'Chief' Notfried's tribal war-band, sworn to lifelong personal loyalty to their lord, but perhaps on the run "... because of some killings ..." as the Norse sagas later delicately express such matters. As duly enrolled as auxiliary legionaries they would have served, ultimately, a Roman commander for whatever term had been agreed with him, and then received the normal 'savings' and reward of land if there was no prior stipulation that they should return home. Returning to their land/s of origin is not part of a standardised pattern, or so we think. If they did do so it was with military experience and their cash savings, a wonder to their countrymen that they should have been paid for only doing what was customary for valiant youths in their own domains! Perhaps our Siegmund is one of their descendants, or even an Anglo-British nephew, who speaks army-Latin, dialect German, and proto-Welsh all with a fluency well adequate for any circumstances likely to involve him, and passes unremarked on market days apart from the little child who notes that he "talks sort of funny."

Nor can we ignore that during whatever actually happened in 367 to be termed The Barbarian Conspiracy, the *Dux Britannorum*, commanding the field army, and the *Comes Litorae Saxoni* in charge of the Saxon Shore forts are Fullofaudes and Nectaridus respectively. Both names are

German – ie 'Saxon' to a Roman – and they belong to the highest military powers in the land. This is 325 years after the Claudian invasion, admittedly, but one does not normally entrust one's army to someone still considered a foreigner because his name might imply dubious loyalty. Whom in more recent times might General Eisenhower and Admiral Nimitz have served had exclusion on such grounds been the rule?

Names, personal trappings, and daily habits are no good guide to very much in any case. Siegmund and Gareth might both have enjoyed a pint of 'Saxon' beer, the barley malted on the adapted hypocaust flooring of an absent rich Roman's somewhat ruinous villa. The beer mugs from which they drank may have been of 'Saxon' design but turned upon a Roman potter's wheel, as at Colchester where presumably there was a ready market for them. They might have worn 'Saxon' style trousers or hose, and kept them up with belt-fastenings developed in Germany for the purpose. Archaeology has found many such fastenings. Quite likely their weaponry, both for hunting and defence, was similar. But nowadays does everyone who enjoys a curry necessarily come from India, or who wears jeans come from USA? By the sixth century we are certainly looking at a considerable population of people who initially were non-Romans, but who had settled in Britannia and who influenced its political course post 410, and probably years earlier, quite noticeably. They were part of the social fabric. So were a fair number of Irish who had settled in the West, most notably in South West Wales, and who seem to have lived by their own particular customs where these suited them, but otherwise become Romanised. Possibly Tewdric himself is descended from these folk, but only if we have unwarranted faith in genealogies. We shall review their reliability soon.

Politically the presence of such a diverse population could well have given Vortigern terrible head-aches, if he found that the settled foreigners did not necessarily take to newcomers from their former lands. Equally these same newcomers might have had traditional/tribal scores to settle with third or subsequent generations of settled 'new' Britons, and a few mini-civil wars on Germanic tribal lines might have erupted. Conceivably Gareth might have been drawn in in support of his pal Siegmund. Certainly the English parts of Britain had begun to coalesce into larger groups as the sixth century progressed. Essex, Sussex, Mercia become recognisable amongst 40 or so others, the smaller of which joined to create larger more viable units for local government. There was neighbourly safety in numbers. During the the same era most of the best land to be had was already settled and worked, not as huge grain-producing fields for tax/feeding the legions, but as smaller mixed-farming units. Archaeology demonstrates this feature, but is unable to show with 100% certainty whether the farmers were Britons or English. And if there had indeed been a sudden influx of 'Saxon' mercenary troops by invitation of Vortigern, they would necessarily have been allocated the land that no-one else was particularly keen to take on, that being all that was available.

They would have noticed this. They may well have objected, and appealed to settled English to help them obtain a better reward for their armed opposition to raiding Picts, Scots, Irish and 'other Saxons'. Conceivably they would have eyed the estates west of the Fosse Way. This scenario is compatible with the traditional view of the results of Vortigern's policy. Old tribal loyalties plus any festering discontents with some *Romanitas* landlords may have prompted a few of the wilder English spirits to join the newcomers in a little warring, raiding and cattle-lifting from the *Romanitas*' estates, and likewise from those who were happy enough to be their prospering tenant-farmers. Young, restless, third or fourth generation Anglo-Britons might have joined in the lawless brigandage resulting; but only after they had got the crops sown on their own long-settled holdings, which were most likely situated east of the Fosse Way. In short, was Vortigern faced by a racial insurrection or an obnoxious degree of lawlessness where the rule of law had long since ceased?

If the latter, the effects would have been mightily unpleasant whilst they lasted, but scarcely enough to justify the hyperbole of the "… groans of the Britons …" addressed to Aetius. Also there may well have been British-English tensions if Gareth noticed that Siegmund was always busy elsewhere if his rowdy nephews were robbing in their mutual vicinity, and urged him to do something to stop them and have them change their ways. Consider what might occur in our own times if the police went on strike. Something akin to this was upsetting the normally decent citizenry at this time, and was blamed on Vortigern, justly or otherwise, as the Boss Man of the day.

The self-regarding citizens of the *Romanitas* party centred west of the Fosse Way would naturally have been alarmed by such mayhem, even if it was not daily threatening them. They had tended to abandon the villa culture in favour of re-occupied, and defensible if necessary, status-displaying, large, olden, Iron-age hill-forts where they became local 'lords of the manor' living richly in new-built wooden halls as a very superior, even kingly, squirearchy. The olden forts may even have given them their superior status; recall Gilbert and Sullivan's Major General who had "... purchased the ancestors in my chapel along with the rest of the estate ..." ("Pirates of Penzance"). And think 'Superior Swiss Chalet' when wood is mentioned, too; people with the skill to build sea-going boats of wooden planks certainly had no need to live in wattle-daub-and-thatch huts. The only trouble is that the archaeology of wood tells us very little of such constructions.

These large landlords maintained their own fighting-men-at arms, as we have noted. They were the natural allies – and possibly relatives – of Ambrosius Aurelianus, and would have felt relieved by the victory at Mount Badon. They may well have seen themselves as 'pure' Romans, too. Vortigern would have appeared to them as a cheap rabble-rouser. Bring back the legions!

And to add to Vortigern's problems there was always the possibility that a couple of real Roman legions might just come roaring in from Gaul, with an ambitious general who would 'rescue' Britannia in the good old fashion before trying to make himself Emperor. We know, with hindsight, that any such spectre for Vortigern was just that. But he probably did not. And throughout all the turmoil, it was still necessary to work the land ... or starve. So long as this was done, the origins of those who farmed it did not matter in the least.

Then came Arthur.

5

Arthur

In view of the two thousand or so 'Arthurian' titles in the specialist library dedicated to him at Mold in Flintshire, it is simplest to let our oldest agreed written source for him speak for itself; –

"Arthur fought against the Saxons alongside the Kings of the Britons, but he himself was the leader in the battles (*dux bellorum*). The first battle was at the mouth of the river which is called Glein. The next four were on the banks of a river which is called Dublglas, and is in the region of Linnius. The sixth was upon the river which is called Bassas. The seventh was in the wood of Celidon; that is Cat Coit Celidon. The eighth was by Castle Guinnion, in which Arthur carried on his shoulders an image of St Mary the Ever-Virgin, and there was a great slaughter of them through the strength of Our Lord Jesus Christ and the Holy Mary his maiden mother. The ninth was in the City of the Legion. The tenth was on the bank of the river which is called Tribuit. The eleventh was on the hill called Agned. The Twelfth was on Mount Badon, in which in one day there fell in one onslaught of Arthur's, nine hundred and sixty men; none slew them but he alone, and in all his battles he remained victor."

Our informant is Nennius, a monk at Bangor-is-y-Coed (*the Monastery below/sheltered by/the Wood*) near Wrexham. In about 822 he wrote a 'Historia Brittonum' in which, "... I have heaped together all that I found, from the Annals of the Romans, the writings of the holy fathers, the Annals of the Irish and the Saxons, and the traditions of our own old men." We have a general idea of the texts he used but cannot be sure

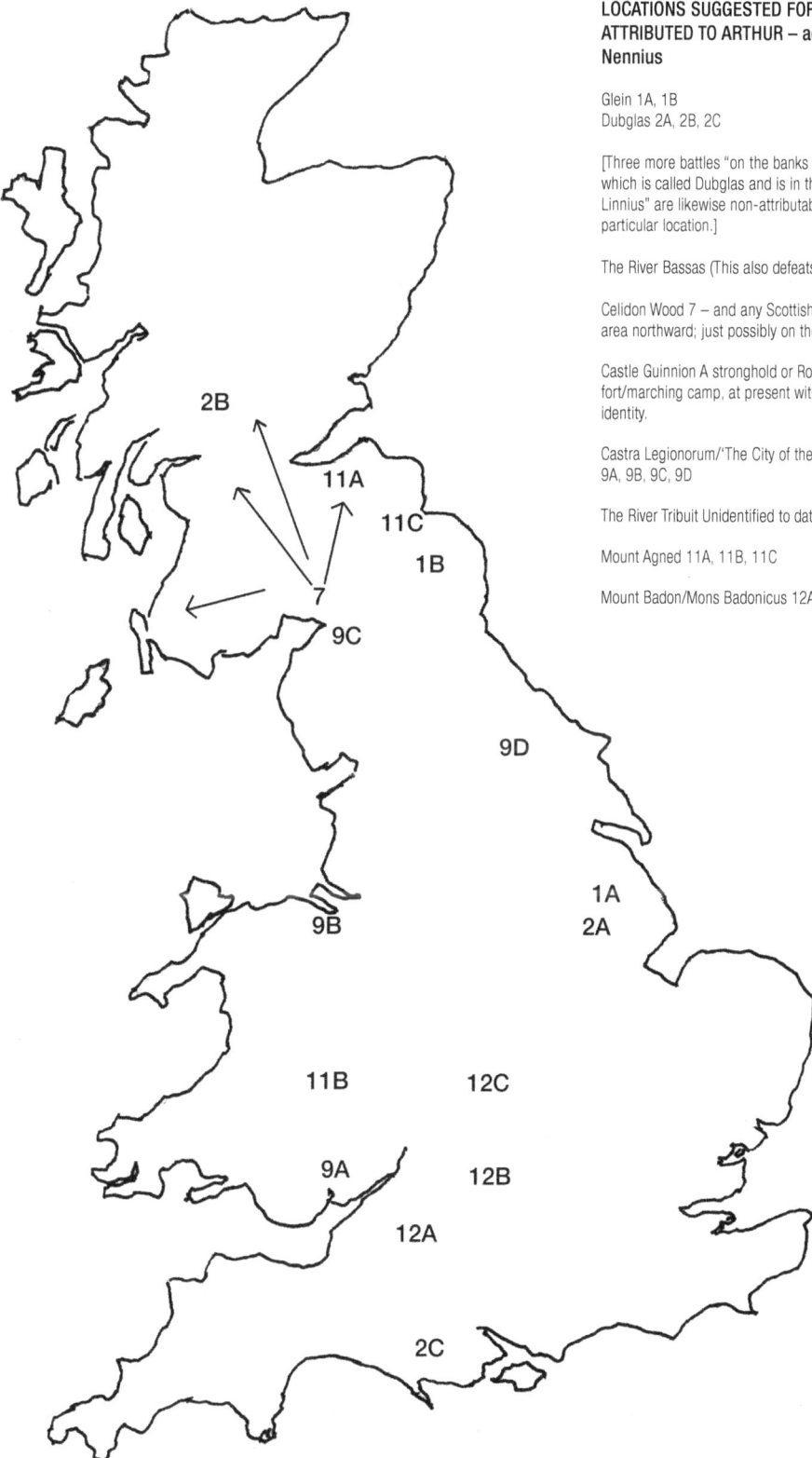

LOCATIONS SUGGESTED FOR BATTLES ATTRIBUTED TO ARTHUR – according to Nennius

Glein 1A, 1B
Dubglas 2A, 2B, 2C

[Three more battles "on the banks of a river which is called Dubglas and is in the region of Linnius" are likewise non-attributable to any particular location.]

The River Bassas (This also defeats location.)

Celidon Wood 7 – and any Scottish Lowlands area northward; just possibly on the upper Clyde.

Castle Guinnion A stronghold or Roman fort/marching camp, at present without plausible identity.

Castra Legionorum/'The City of the Legions' 9A, 9B, 9C, 9D

The River Tribuit Unidentified to date.

Mount Agned 11A, 11B, 11C

Mount Badon/Mons Badonicus 12A, 12B, 12C

what versions/copies of them he actually perused. Much has 'gone missing' and only a portion of the copies of these sources, made before and since his time, is with us now. With the fruits of our own researches to hand we can find fault with him quite often. However, he deserves to be viewed as an honest man, clearly thinking of himself as Welsh, who was sincerely doing his best to enlighten all who read him. So long as we remember that he is writing a good 300 years after the time of Arthur he is worth our attention. He also tells us one additional great truth about Arthur; he is "Arthur the soldier. There were many more noble than he."

This statement knocks on the head any idea of 'King' Arthur. Subsequent to his probable campaigning times, judged to have been from the late fifth into the early sixth centuries, there were King Arthurs appearing in several Welsh genealogies, doubtless reflecting his fame. But it does not seem that Arthur had any claim to royalty. He is thought to have been killed in action at Camlann in 537/539. The great battle of Mount Badon attributed to him by Nennius can be dated c490 – 518 depending upon which source one uses. Therefore we could risk dating his birth to the late 460s, when Ambrosius Aurelianus is quelling the disturbances of the Vortigern era, and has St Gildas grant the Mount Badon victory to him and never mention Arthur. If Mount Badon is one of the hills around Bath it is strategically possible that there were in fact two battles there, thus permitting such a span of dates, but frankly we do not know the truth of the matter. Nennius and Gildas cannot both be right about the date if just one battle was fought and won by *Romanitas* oriented troops who crushed the enemy at this unknown location.

What do we make of the title 'Dux Bellorum'? It translates neatly enough as 'Leader of Wars'. Is this what it meant to Nennius, though, or is he translating into Latin a title he has heard from the recitations of Welsh Bards, something along the lines of "ameraudur llywiaudir llawur" (*general, emperor, battle-ruler)* or "tywyssawc cat" (*leader of the host, army, battle)*? In this case what might the Bards have meant? Much paper, ink, fire and fury have been expended in trying to find out defini- tively, but we are no further forward for our present purposes. 'Dux' also translates as 'Duke', and is a late Roman senior military rank or title. Was this being applied consciously to Arthur by Nennius? Goodness knows! We must be content with the gist of our obvious translation of 'War Leader', a supreme commander of forces in any particular campaign. It also appears that he was highly successful, unless Nennius has judged twelve battles to be an honourable number, conjured them up from somewhere willy-nilly, and put Arthur in charge of the campaigns which culminated in them. Has Nennius' Welsh patriotism got the better of his judgement, he having "... taken the trouble of writing down a few fragments which refute the stupidity of the British race (of which they are accused) because their learned men had no knowledge and had not written in books any record of that island of Britain ... But I have heaped together ..."? And so he has, bless him! For all its quirks his work is one of our few records of the period.

Let us look at Nennius' – though perhaps not entirely Arthur's – battles and see if we can learn from them anything that might give us clues about Arthur, Dux Bellorum. The logic of so doing is perfect, but as soon as we get out our Ordnance Survey maps and the AA/RAC gazetteers we find that the names known to Nennius no longer apply. Also if Camlann, Arthur's last battle, was fought in 537/9, plenty of time had elapsed since a Mount Badon victory in 490 for the 'Camlann Arthur' to have been a young blood whose *Romanitas* parents had named him in honour of 'Mount Badon Arthur'. Would Nennius have spotted such a possibility? It is doubtful. Arthur is his hero; thus all Arthurian battles were to be attributed to him. We have no reliable texts to help us cross-check such possibilities, moreover. However, Camlann as a location is pretty securely traced to a fort on Hadrian's Wall, *Camboglanna,* which now bears the name Birdoswald. In early English this may mean a wood which was owned by, or quite near the dwelling of, one Birdo or Birda. But the 'English' name does not look at all like Camlann. And so it is with the rest of the battles. If we set out scholarship's multiple best guesses the result is thus;-

1)   River Glein – in Lincolnshire or Northumberland.
2–5) River Dubglas – in Lincolnshire, or a stream which runs into Loch Lomond via Glen Douglas, or a stream in Dorset.
6)   River Bassas – defeats all ingenuity.
7)   Celidon Wood – anywhere from Carlisle northwards.

8)   Castle Guinnion – a fort of pre-Roman antiquity, or a Roman castra; neither currently identified.
9)   City of the Legions – Caerleon, or Chester, or York, or Carlisle, or another Roman base. 10) River Tribuit – so far unidentified.
11)   Mount Agned – the Venerable Bede suggested Edinburgh; add on Leintwardine (Herefordshire), or High Rochester (Cheviot Hills)
12)   Mount Badon – Bath, Lincolnshire, Swindon, Badbury.

The problem is obvious, even if we trust Nennius. Arthur fought all over the land it seems. And perhaps he did.

The best we can do, with a couple of exceptions – chiefly the 'City of the Legions' options – is to note that these suggestions for the location of his battles cluster very roughly along the Fosse Way and Hadrian's Wall. If we dare go thus far in any assertion upon the matter we can say that they are 'frontier' engagements. The east of the island of Britain seems clear of Arthur's attention, or at least that of his employers. Have 250 years or so of quiet and moderately peaceful 'Saxon' settlement east of the Fosse Way set up the basis for England as a land of prospering yeoman farmers descended from a variety of original tribes and nations? Is Arthur employed only by the Kings of the large western estates, proud of their *Romanitas* and defending their ex-Imperial holdings against all comers and despoilers, speaking Welsh rather than Latin, and drawing upon pre-Roman traditions and genealogies to create status for themselves and justification for their way of life? Are they Christian, however nominally, into the bargain? Are they deliberately not preaching the Gospel to the 'Saxons', for which omission St Gildas chides them, but are withholding it in a spirit of vengeful spite which they hope will see all English consigned to hellfire upon their deaths? Are they, in the pride of their idiosyncratic developing culture, turning in upon themselves in their world view and feeling all the more superior and comforted thereby?

As we have wondered, what would anyone in Arthur's Britain find in the old Roman-Imperial ideal which was worth fighting for? The average Briton west of the Fosse Way would have wanted peace and stability; leading citizens would beyond doubt be occupied with affairs of their own, and be in arms occasionally to advance and defend them. So far as Arthur is concerned we are viewing independent Kings of Britain, looking after their own interests and hiring Arthur and his troops as the best fighting force available to them to put experience and extra muscle behind the efforts of their own retainers. The enemy was not necessarily 'Saxon,' Pict, Scot, or any other racial grouping, but anyone who stood in the way of these aristocrats' personal ambitions. There was no central authority and accompanying rule of law to which they could turn for justice and redress if they felt themselves wronged. What they wanted they either took, and held on to if they could, or went without. They were, whether they so regarded themselves or not, the 'Cymru', the 'comrades'/'companions in arms' when pursuing interests common to them all as the fledgling Welsh nation. And we must instantly qualify this a good deal; Wales did not exist in 500. It did by circa 600, but still included Lancashire, Cumbria, and some additional land to the north, Devon, Cornwall, and sundry odd enclaves where English ways of organising life had not yet been adopted. Later such ways might be imposed by conquest as the English kingdoms – still basically east of the Fosse Way – grew, centralised, and became effective in all Departments of State, taxes and wars included.

These are very sweeping statements, and open to justifiable criticism from many angles. But broadly it is the way Britain was being shaped; English lowlands and Celtic fringes.

Meanwhile Arthur – the Bear – and his band of trained, disciplined, fully equipped, and well drilled fighting men were available for hire by the *Romanitas* Kings. His troops cannot have been many in number, say 40 at a generous estimate. The expense of maintaining such a body from year to year would be considerable. If they were mounted, if only for transport and logistical purposes, their horses – likely Exmoor Pony type stock – would have added to the cost of maintaining them. The celebrated Roman road network would still have been in pretty good shape, certainly better than anything enjoyed by, say, Henry VIII, and movement over distances quite easy for these troops accordingly. From Nennius' battle list, if we are to trust it, Arthur operated extensively along the frontiers of the British kingdoms, so the extra speed and carrying capacity of horses would have helped him to appear rapidly and unexpectedly at the location of any trouble and nip it in the bud, before opportunistic plundering by any locally disaffected elements spread and added to the looting and chaos.

Nor let us forget that the cause of such flare-ups could just as likely have been a *Romanitas* king flexing his muscles, as a raid from beyond his frontiers or from across the sea. Arthur may be considered a mercenary, perhaps even of 'Saxon' descent. Such an unheroic status, embarrassing to some *Romanitas* kingly allies, could well explain why St Gildas does not mention him, and why the Church is not his staunchest supporter either. Arthur knew his worth and had his price. Those who needed his services, ecclesiastical, lay, or both in combination, paid it or were left to fend for themselves. We do not know whether or not he and his men ever fought upon horseback; we recall Hnaudifridius and his 'numerus' operating as auxiliary light cavalry on Hadrian's wall. Perhaps Arthur had learned about some tactics from such a quarter, although the idea that he imported large horses from Frisia and mounted a squadron of armoured knights upon them is about as likely as Riothamus' two legions. Bards later praising and enhancing his prowess have done him no favours in terms of accurate history.

The vast literature upon Arthurian themes will satisfy those who wish to pursue him and his career. It has no direct bearing upon St Tewdric, and could be ignored in relation to him if the document known to us as the 'Jesus College Pedigree (9)' did not record a line of succession to the throne of Morgannwg thus; – Erb – Nynniaw – Llywarch – Tewdric – Meurig – Arthrwys – Morgan – and continuing . . . It is the occurrence of the name Arthrwys which immediately catches the eye, and has caught the eyes of various researchers into 'Arthurian' times likewise. In the absence of reliable dates, which issue we must later tackle along with the reliability or otherwise of genealogies in general, a leap of faith has often been made between King Arthrwys of Morgannwg and 'King' Arthur, despite Nennius' denial of his royalty.

The Iron-Age hill fort of Llanmelin, situated on the edge of the Wentwood a mile or so north of Caerwent, has been chosen by some enthusiasts as Camelot. Some odd outworks at its eastern end are, to such as they, 'obviously' the stables for his knights' horses. In fact

Llanmelin translates 'Llan' – an enclosure, 'Melin' (cf Latin *molere* = to grind) a mill. It is more probable that Camelot owes something to Camulos, a British god of war from pre-Roman times, about whom practically nothing is known beyond the name 'Camulodunum' (= the 'ground sacred to Camulos') which occurs both at Colchester and also in the vicinity of Slack a little north-east of Preston. Quite possibly there are others, undiscovered or unpublicised. Thanks to Nennius we have seen how names can be duplicated in different places around the country, change over time, and have local variants in spelling and pronunciation. In this way it is not difficult, if one is so inclined, to find Arthurian associations all over Britain, and it was just such a surge of enthusiasm in the 1980s which pushed Mathern and St Tewdric into the limelight.

A strange conviction seemed to have developed during those days that a Celtic (and what does Celtic mean, exactly? Cultural traits? Language? Art? Mystical insights?) 'Golden Age' had been all around us in Wales, unnoticed, unhonoured, and most especially vibrant along the lower lands of Glamorgan and Gwent/Monmouthshire. Its rediscovery, exhibition, and development would somehow bring about a vast renaissance of old, hidden mysteries and Celtic lore. There was on hand a supply of material for wonders which would dwarf more established places of interest like Stonehenge and the Tower of London. Cardiff airport would need to be developed beyond anything dreamed of in terms of extra runways for London Heathrow, in order to deal with the world's touristic interest in such attractions as the tomb of King Arthur, which had just been discovered in a ruined church upon a hilltop conveniently in central Glamorgan. This was in the summer of 1983. An approach was made to the Welsh Development Authority for a sum of money sufficient to improve the airport, widen some roads, and provide hotels and 'interpretative facilities' at the tomb's site. Among enthusiasts the excitement knew no bounds, and when the WDA proved rightly cautious about committing any public money to such schemes until their bases had been authenticated by every competent authority, astounding headlines blazed in the Welsh press, and the Arthurian myths received their best airing since the Middle Ages.

As we have seen, there is a genealogical connection for Tewdric – Meurig – Arthrwys, and this brought great interest to Mathern where St Tewdric is buried in the church dedicated to him. Meurig, according to the Celtic enthusiasts, has fared rather better, with his tomb situated somewhere close to the altar in Llandaff cathedral. In that tomb, ran one assertion, Meurig would be found wrapped in the hide of a stag, its skull incorporated into his helmet, and bearing – all within the same coffin, presumably – antlers of twelve tines, one for each Apostle, for he was of a Christian dynasty. But since Llandaff was unsure of this tomb's location, and was less than enthusiastic about beginning instant excavations to locate it, why should not the same rites of interment have been afforded to his father, St Tewdric? He had ended his days as a Christian hermit so, beyond all Celtic doubt, he would have antlers too. Dig him up, therefore!

The shock suffered by a couple of amiable elderly ladies, engaged in arranging the flowers in the church at Mathern, when some ardent Celts appeared one afternoon and demanded to be shown the "hidden documents" which related to Tewdric's grave, can well be imagined. Having rampaged, ranted and roared for a while, they eventually went on their way, but were back again at the end of the main service the following Sunday when a more historically informed Churchwarden was on hand, although still ignorant of the 'discovery' of Arthur's tomb. The best on offer to them then was a suggestion to look in a reference library for Fred Hando's report of his visit to Mathern in 1946, and what the lady had told him. A denial of any hidden documents, the information that all the old parish archives were in any case held at the National Library of Wales at Aberystwyth, plus a flat refusal to countenance any digging unless under the auspices of Cadw and the National Museum of Wales, sent these enthusiasts on their way making most unpleasant remarks about the English ... in vivid Anglo-Saxon parlance.

The 'Celtic Renaissance' had soon found its way overseas, and all sorts of people, some calm, scholarly and sincere, others pursuing personal or commercial aims of one sort or another, made their views known locally well into the 1990s. By this time we at Mathern knew that the historical and archaeological bases for such Celtic claims was rather slight, and that there was nothing here which would ever satisfy the wilder ideas voiced.

Some of these were becoming a nuisance, in fact. From the plains of Central USA came a wondrous proposal, offered by a group which appeared to be a cross between a sort of secret society and an amateur dramatic troupe. It proposed to enter into a partnership with St Tewdric's church on the basis that the church should be "properly displayed and marketed", that an American franchise should handle all souvenirs, that car parking fees should be shared between the church and the secret society – once all "administrative expenses" had been deducted – and much more of the same kind, this generous offer standing for three months following the date on the letter. The signature that this missive bore was that of the incumbent "White Rod Bearer of the Right Hand Quadrant in the Mystic Vortex of The Golden Eternity ..." and a bit more besides, now forgotten, but all printed in blue and golden Gothic lettering at the head of the paper.

A delightful aerial picture postcard of Chepstow castle was sent him by way of reply, stating simply, "MATHERNA NON EST TERRA DISNEYIS NEC TEWDRICUS SANCTUS REXQUE MICHAELILLUS MUS." We heard no more from him.

Decency and common sense duly returned. Local historical societies throughout South Wales took issue with the general tenor of the Celtic claims, and informed opinion looked increasingly askance upon 'proofs' such as King Arthur's Tombstone. This, for published purposes, consisted of a photograph of a flat piece of rock upon which was written/incised "REX ARTORIVS FILI MAVRICIVS" the genitive case and the progenitor having become a little mixed in those Celtic Dark Ages, perhaps. And no competent people were allowed to examine the stone, either. In 1992 some particular enthusiasts were cleared of stealing paintings then valued at £40,000 from St Donat's chapel, though one of them admitted having received them; they had been found under his bed, he having bought them from a man in a pub. Perhaps the last straw in the Arthurian wind landed heavily when an apparently genuine Iron-Age 'La Tene' culture sword was found, stratigraphically, to be of more recent date than a length of precisely datable 1940s barbed wire which lay at a good depth below it in ground excavated by the 'Time Team' popular TV archaeological programme. Phil Harding, an expert 'digging' archaeologist, looked sadly at the camera and spoke words recalled thus, "Well, I've got to be careful what I say here, I suppose, but let's just say that it looks as though this sword went into the ground within living memory . . ."

Celtic Arthurianism of the 1980s/'90s, viewed from Mathern, had been a sad and bad affair all round.

Not all research of the period has been squalid, however. A local government official, Chris Barber, who had a special responsibility for Gwent's Countryside Warden Service, produced a number of excellent guide books detailing ancient and interesting locations of history and legend throughout Wales. 'Mysterious Wales' and 'More Mysterious Wales' are titles which come readily to mind. The latter outlines some of the enthusiastic Celtic claims, and does so with no particular comment or bias, attributing all statements to their sources. He has also turned his attention to Arthur, as opposed to King Arthrwys, and advances the intriguing idea that Arthur did not die at Camlann, although subsequently some other individual named Arthur could have done. Arthur himself, he writes, followed the same path as Tewdric; retired and became a hermit, went to Brittany, and died there peacefully, his tomb being located in the village of St Armel. Further, his bloodline lives on, his direct descendant being a Mr. Williams who is a 'City Gent' occupied in the financial institutions of the City of London. Lecturing to The Chepstow Society in September 2018, Chris Barber assured his audience that when he told Mr Williams of his lineage, ". . . he took it very well." It does not appear, though, that Mr. Williams will be seeking to dethrone the Royal House of Windsor at any time soon.

And upon this happier note, let us proceed to dates and genealogies.

6

Dates and Genealogies ...

"Once upon a time, a long time ago ..." begins many a good old story. The tale of Tewdric's last battle comes well and truly into this category. It was a significant event. Its outcome mattered; indeed it set the Welsh border on the lower Wye where it remains. Is this not enough by which to remember him? Three cheers for good old Tewdric, therefore! But then comes the awkward historian, an Englishman in the present case, who asks, "*Who* was the enemy? *When* did this happen? *Why* was Meurig apparently late on the scene? *Why* is Tewdric buried six miles away at Mathern? *What* is all this business about stags and a cart? *Why* do 'fountains' and wells appear important in the narrative?" And so on, probing away to get as much detail from the story as it possibly may yield.

We noted earlier (Chapter 2) that the names Tewdric and Meurig are *Romanitas* in tone. Following the *Romanitas* trail we noted that there were two Roman Emperors reigning at the sort of time when a powerful Briton – fast becoming Y Cymro (*a Welshman*) – might have liked to have been associated with *Romanitas* to reinforce his legitimate possession of the ex-Roman estates his forbears had appropriated. With such a suspicion in mind we can consider possible dates for this choice of names. The de-facto 'Western' Roman Emperor, Theoderic the Ostrogoth who occupied Italy, reigned 493-526, and the Eastern Emperor Maurice, at Constantinople, reigned 582-602. What better names for a Welsh king to conjure with if he wished to show himself as a *Romanitas* supporter of his times' status quo? Therefore, what times were these?

Within the span of Theoderic's reign Ambrosius Aurelianus was eliminating the last vestiges of such violence and chaos as were subsequently laid at Vortigern's door. Indeed, if we take St Gildas' hint at a date, 490, the battle of Mount Badon had already been fought and won by the *Romanitas* Party, though this still leaves scope for Arthur maybe to have to do it again in 516/18. So *Romanitas* was the flavour-of-the-day. Give one's child a Roman name, therefore. This may provide us with a good indication for Tewdric's lifetime assuming – as we may – that Tewdric was a baby's given name, and not a name taken by a mature man at his adult baptism having become a Christian convert. The same considerations apply to Meurig, who succeeds him. A Roman name, a Christian profession in religious matters, a martial backing for his grip on power, and a long and peaceful reign, are all Meurig's attributes.

We should not overlook the role of the Church in these times. There remains just a possibility that Christianity never completely died away after the legions withdrew. There is some evidence for this locally at Caerwent. A pewter bowl with a scratched "Chi-ro" upon it was found by archaeologists in a context suggestive of its having been hidden away, perhaps during Diocletian's persecution of Christians in 303. In 313 Constantine the Great made Christianity a legal religion throughout the Empire; what a difference a decade can make! Therefore, a Christian culture of belief and practice at household level had possibly lingered on in some form or other, to be given a resurgence by Christian contacts with Brittany and, later, a new Church in Ireland where St Patrick was active from about 432 onwards. Like so much else about this period, it is unwise to generalise too much about what was taking place.

It is also occasionally asked, often with an implied sneer, "If King Tewdric was such a splendid Christian, what awful violence had he done in his earlier life to suggest to him the wisdom of ending his mortal life as a conspicuously holy hermit in hope of getting a swift passage through the pearly gates of Heaven? Aren't Christians supposed to love their neighbours and do good to those who hate them?" Most certainly, and if one should have the responsibilities of a ruler, one's first duties in love for one's people are to protect them from molestation by enemies, to administer justice, and give good law within one's realm. The Book of Llandaff opens its Tewdric record by making just these points. It seems that Tewdric had done all this well, and both loved and cared for his people, setting a good example to fellow contemporary rulers.

In strictly historical terms, so far as we may now discern them, Tewdric could have been descended from the Silures, a fierce and combative British tribe which had given the invading Romans a rough time. Eventually they were 'civilised' in the Venta Silurum, now Caerwent, from which the county of Gwent derives its name. It would also have encompassed the land which supplied Isca, the *Castra Legionis* – now Caerleon on the river Usk – its necessary rations to keep the troops of the Second Augusta Legion fed when at full regimental strength there. Other productive lands lay to the west of the Usk in an 'estate' known as Glywyseg, which seems to have been incorporated into Tewdric's realm towards the end of the sixth century, expanding his territory markedly. The name Morgannwg for an even larger area could derive from the activities of Meurig and his heirs during the seventh century and, if this is so, should not correctly be applied to Tewdric's times. Perhaps the Book of Llandaff is in error here. That any of this expansion was accomplished without some bloodshed in the process is unlikely. We, however, know only the final outcome, not the contemporary context. Beyond doubt, though, a good and Christian king had to take up arms occasionally to assert himself for his people.

We may here recall that St Germanus/St Garmon had followed an administrative career in Roman Gaul and Britanny before having the Bishopric of Auxerre thrust upon him as someone literate and experienced in administration, military measures included. He came to Britannia and visited St Illtud at his monastery of Llantwit Major, leaving a legacy of learning which later educated St Gildas, as we have noted. However, in 429 he was called upon in a decidedly secular capacity. Let us allow the Venerable St Bede (c 673-735) to take up the story; "... The Saxons and the Picts had joined forces and made war upon the Britons, whom necessity had compelled to arm ... they (the Britons) called upon the saintly Bishop for help ... Germanus promised to direct the battle in person. He picked out the most active men, and having surveyed the surrounding country, observed a valley among the hills lying in the direction from which he expected the enemy to approach. Here he stationed the untried forces under his own orders, and gave instructions that directly the main body of their remorseless enemies came within sight of those whom he had placed in ambush, they were to join him in a mighty shout when he raised his standard. The enemy advanced confidently, expecting to take the Britons unawares; whereupon the Bishop shouted three times, "Hallelujah!" The whole army joined in the shout until the surrounding hills echoed with the sound. The enemy column panicked, thinking the very rocks and sky were falling on them, and were so terrified that they could not run fast enough. Throwing away their weapons in headlong flight, they were well content to escape naked …" Well done, St Germanus! You are justly famous for your 'Hallelujah War', if rather neglected otherwise.

To modern eyes this episode has something of a miraculous Old Testament blood-and-thunder fantastical feeling to it, as when "Joshua fit the battle of Jericho / An' the walls came a-tumblin' down …" Now, we know Jericho's walls collapsed, twice in fact, but not at times when Joshua was likely to have been in the vicinity. There is a problem there. But this is not so at Moy in Invernesshire in 1746. Moy is situated about a dozen miles south of Inverness, and until North Sea Oil days the main road between Inverness and the south of Scotland ran through it in a very narrow and steep-sided valley. In February 1746 Prince Charles Edward Stuart, the 'Young Pretender' – 'Bonnie Prince Chairlie' of song and romantic legend – withdrew his demoralised and diminishing army northwards along this road towards Inverness, with no clear plan but to evade the greater forces of George II, King of Great Britain and Hanover, which were relentlessly closing in upon it.

The Young Pretender stopped at Moy at the house of Lady Anne Mackintosh, the Lady of Moy, 'La Belle Rebelle', Jacobite wife of The Mackintosh of Moy. This laird and Clan Chieftain was himself a staunch Royalist and government supporter, but at the time he was away with King George's forces in the northwest of Scotland keeping a grip on the Isles. Whatever the true political sympathies of this seemingly ill-matched pair may have been, it is very evident that regardless of the rebellion's outcome there would still be a Mackintosh of Moy governing the Clan Mackintosh estates! This aspect to the situation aside, Bonnie Prince

Chairlie felt himself secure as La Belle Rebelle's house guest for a night or so. His army was encamped to the south, and there were naturally a few picket out-posts and sentries stationed in and around the valley. But La Belle Rebelle thought little of their effectiveness. Accordingly she summoned her estate blacksmith and four sturdy clansmen, armed them to the teeth, and sent them out into the winter's night to reconnoitre towards Inverness, which General Lord Loudon held for King George. The Prince's own sentries and outposts were found to have long since taken shelter from the elements, and were to that degree ineffectual in the densest parts of the valley's woods. This was just what Lord Loudon, who had had word of the Prince's presence, had foreseen. As darkness fell he set out with a small force to pay Moy a visit.

The blacksmith and his companions, by then on the road in the valley's floor below the shivering sentries, and moving cautiously through the darkness in the direction of Inverness, came upon Loudon's force. Braw Highland bravado, and no little courage, inspired the blacksmith to loose off a musket shot at it. The story goes that the ball killed Loudon's piper who, given the stealthy needs of the hour, can scarcely have been playing at the time. Alarm and panic seized the Royal troops, and when the four Moy clansmen fired in their turn they halted and prepared to run. The Blacksmith shouted the Moy battle cry (*sluagh-ghairm* = slogan) possibly reloaded in the dark and fired again, all this noise waking up the Prince's outposts around and above him. They, not to be outdone, roared out their own clans' slogans, and popped off a few shots into the night, whereupon the blacksmith switched to speaking English and loudly ordered any number of named Highland rebel regiments to "... go and slaughter these dogs ..." As perceived by Loudon's force every clan in the Prince's whole army was bellowing from the slopes above them, and they quickly decided to pass the night safely back in Inverness. The Prince awoke and came outside into the freezing cold, prepared to flee if necessary, and caught a severe chill.

We see in both these accounts the common factors of surprise, ill-discipline, lack of leadership on the part of one force, individual fear spurring instincts of self-preservation, the panic spreading, and a largely bloodless rout resulting. So let us not dismiss lightly brief reports of events from long ago, however unlikely they may seem. We usually do not have enough knowledge of their contexts to pass more than the most tentative of judgements upon them. Well done, Saint Germanus!

As for our dating Tewdric and Meurig by reference to reigning Roman Emperors, we may tentatively suggest the following;-

526	Death of Emperor Theoderic.
520–526 /7	Birth of Tewdric?
582	Accession of Eastern Emperor Maurice.
582	onwards – Birth of Meurig?
590–600	Death of Tewdric, following a battle by the Wye.
circa 650	Meurig's gift of the 'Manor' of Mathern to the Bishop of Llandaff; perhaps as a legacy at his death.

These dates require Tewdric to be quite elderly when he fathered Meurig, and for Meurig himself to have been in his teens when the battle at Tintern was fought, but they are not beyond the limits of our tradition. Also, Meurig's youth could explain his absence from the fighting without shame to him or his later reputation.

Another way to try to date Tewdric to the context of a particular historical period is to turn to the genealogies which were so important in a more or less non-literate society, and to allocate arbitrarily a span of 30 years reign to each of the kings mentioned in them. This is a rough and ready method, but in the absence of a better indication it can give a useful clue or so around which to work. The trouble is that our information here is derived from the tales of bards, whom the great and powerful supported in order to add to their fame and glory, but not to tell everything in accurate detail. A fully true narrative could have been embarrassing if some royal personage had had 'lapses' every time he saw an attractive woman or a full amphora of wine. No bard could make a living, or even live very long, if he told unwelcome truths. Thus he had to weave a gaudy tapestry of his times, gilding all lilies (remember Riothamus' two legions?) and pleasing all who heard him recite. He would have been something of a musician, too, chanting his narratives as he plucked upon a small harp, somewhat akin to a lyre, if we are guided by the Saxon remains of an instrument from the Sutton Hoo ship burial, and a few manuscript illustrations of angels in full accompanied song. Our nearest modern equivalent might be a rap singer with a banjo.

But surely our history of Tewdric is written in a solemn source, the 'Book of Llandaff'? Can it only derive from the effusions of a bard? It seems so. A bardic treatment is discernible behind the transcription of the 'Tale of Tewdric' into the Book's uneven Latin. The form of a Tale chanted for entertainment in a lordly hall is clear. First come the boasts of the old warrior king as war looms; then follows a miraculous occurrence (for Celtic literature abounds with wonders and fantastic deeds and events); then comes a battle, an account of the action, and an unclerical interest in spoils and plunder; next very ancient wonders attend the hero's death. It is all there, just as we might expect.

Its original audience would have known just what to expect, too, and the Bard would have looked around the hall to sum up his audience. He had to please, modifying his act as necessary to achieve this essential outcome. His audience would have wanted to hear of their own deeds of prowess, and also of those of their ancestors and kinsmen. This was the way history was transmitted. So great and glorious deeds prevailed, and the exact sequence of dates could be bent to include as many of these as possible in the narrative. Further, the audience would have known who was related to whom, or claimed plausibly to be so (cf the many 'sons' of Emperor Macsen Wledig) and preened themselves on being seated in such illustrious company as of right. They expected the Bard to note them, their ancestry, their prestigious connections, and include them in his narration, then and subsequently. In this way the Bard would have given everyone his due, but left those less well-informed, ourselves included, in something of a daze as we try to piece together a true chronology to date, and so clarify, the history of those days.

Let us construct a make-believe genealogy, the better to illustrate this difficulty.

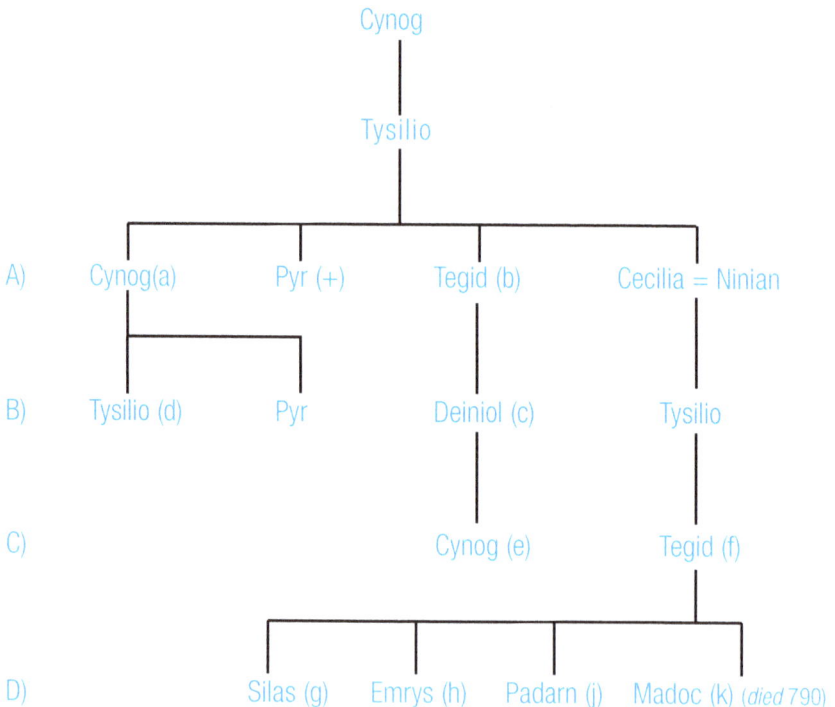

Our 'Royal Family' starts with King Cynog succeeded by King Tysilio, who begin the family tree.

In the first generation (A) following King Tysilio, there reigned King Cynog (a). His brother Pyr (+) became a monk and had no children. Their brother Tegid (b) was the father of Deiniol (c), and their sister Cecilia married Ninian, a prince from another kingdom, who became in due course the father of Tysilio who reigned in his due course as king of that kingdom and was the father of Tegid(f). Meanwhile King Tegid (b) died whilst his surviving heirs were still children, and the crown passed to King Deiniol (c). He died whilst his heir Cynog (e) was still in his cradle, and his cousin Tysilio (d) inherited the crown. His brother Pyr had died in infancy, and upon reaching maturity Prince Cynog (e) considered he should be the rightful king. King Tysilio (d) having his own ideas on the subject, unwisely accepted an invitation from Prince Cynog (e) to join him on a hunting expedition . . . from which King Cynog (e) returned, his uncle having met with an unfortunate accident – so said the Coroner's jury – whilst engaged in the chase. The Queen of King Tysilio (d), whose name has not come down to us, unlike her shameful end, was noted to be something of a pharmacist, and King Cynog (e) died of a septic bee sting she was treating, but not before condemning her as a witch who was duly drowned in a weighted sack.

There the dynasty might have ended, had not young King Tegid (f) responded to the entreaties of King Cynog (e)'s widow, and accepted the Crown, and her hand in wedlock. All went well for 30 years or so, until King Tegid (f) died peacefully of old age, and Prince Silas (g) succeeded him. King Silas (g) shortly afterwards disappeared without trace whilst helping a desperate neighbouring king cull a surplus of ravaging dragons. No better luck attended King Emrys (h) and Prince Padarn (j), the latter reigning " . . . for but as long as a hunter might hold his bow at full draw . . . " whilst likewise out dragon culling. King Madoc (k) a man of strong principles, declined to hunt dragons out of season, and spent a winter in deep thought upon pest control and which pests should be controlled as a priority. A sudden spring raid by himself and a mounted force of picked warriors he had quietly recruited through the usual channels during the winter, despatched the importunate and dragon-afflicted neighbouring king, and found no dragons to cull once this worthy's ability to detect them was no longer available to hunters. King Madoc (k) took over this neighbouring kingdom whilst his warrior force was still on hand, and found that his new frontier was along the Dyke of King Offa of Mercia (reigned 757-796) and also 'Bretwalda' – acknowledged supremely powerful king – in all England. Appreciating the etiquette to be observed when one was neighbour to such a poten-tial ally, or source of anguish, King Madoc took pains that year to deliver King Offa's Christmas present in person. King Offa, who recognised a wise man when he met one, was full of seasonal good humour and goodwill, and granted King Madoc the honour of witnessing a charter he was signing for the endowment of a monastery. The occasion overwhelmed poor Madoc, alas, "... et proximo die mortus est, id est in festa Sancti Stephani anno DCCXC ..." commemorated one of the chartered monks.

So this long, doleful and confusing tale at last yields us a date, Boxing Day 790. From this we can work backwards to find out roughly when King Cynog lived. Can we, though? To clarify our narrative in this present telling, all reigning kings have been given 'labels' (a), (b), (c) and so on to help the reader. Although sometimes a monarch has a sobriquet, eg '... the bald', '... the bold', '... the big-bellied' to aid identification, these are the exception. The bard's audience knew all about the people of whom he chanted; we do not. We have instead 3 Cynogs, 3 Tysilios, 2 Pyrs, and 2 Tegids, and even when writing became more common and written genealogies confirmed, for example, 'Tegid ap Tysilio', it was often not clear how they fitted into any particular pedigree. In our invented kingdom we have four generations, A), B), C), D). If we allow 30 years for each, we can 'go back' 120 years from 790, and arrive at roughly the right period to consider. If, however, we take each reigning king as successor in due natural course of time to his predecessor, and again apply 30 years to each name, we total 360 years, and the result is nonsense even if it looks plausible here and there.

Therefore beware of genealogies. The bards of old were just as capable of filling in gaps in their knowledge, or 'improving' upon hazy memories, as we are. Material we have received from bardic sources is useful to tell us of the thoughts and attitudes of a particular time, but it must be handled with great care.

Now let us range truly fantastical.

7

Great Wonders

We have suggested that the tradition of Tewdric's final battle and death as recorded in the Book of Llandaff is based upon a bardic recitation. Apart from being briefed the night before the battle by "... the Angel of the Lord ..." Tewdric has his personal ambulance drawn by two stags "... yoked and ready before the house where he lodged ..." with refreshing springs bubbling up wherever this carriage halted en route to "... the island of Echni ..." (most likely Flat Holm) "... the place which I have desired where I shall like to lie after death ..." These embellishments give colour to the bald facts of history, such as they may be in this case, but also they provide that extra dimension of mystery and wonder, a realm of 'Other' than customary 3D + Time of day-to-day life, and very much beloved by the Celtic culture and the various peoples embracing it.

This underlying realm of the supernatural pervades and enriches a mental community far beyond specific localities and times. It is mystical, immaterial, and awesome, yet with its own virtues of correct conduct and observance in response to the power of the changing seasons and the varied associated cycles of all that lives. It is old as Creation itself, and the barely sensed bedrock of consciousness for all who heard Tewdric's tale chanted in the firelit halls of the great personages of the age. We must consider it in order to hear, absorb, and understand these times as far as we may, and learn of them accordingly, the better to inform and enliven our own.

St Tewdric's Church, Mathern

St Tewdric

St Tewdric (Sculpture by Neil Gow)

St Tewdric's Well, Mathern

St Tewdric's Well, Mathern

St Clydawg's Church, Clodock

St Clydawg's Well

St Clydawg's Well

Let us contemplate the stags, "yoked and ready", provided by some power from the realm of 'Other' for the specific purpose of taking the dying king to his chosen resting place. Certainly they are in the service of God, but is God here exactly as conceived by the Abrahamic traditions of Torah, Bible, and Qur'an? It seems not so. At best our story tells of the old spiritual perception engaged in the service of the new Christian revelation. This point is well made in local legend by the circumstances surrounding the arrival of St Tathan (*Tadeus*) at Caerwent to evangelize and found his monastery there, somewhat before Tewdric's reign. As already stated, Caerwent had had a Christian presence from the fourth century, so perhaps Tathan was fanning up embers which were still smouldering quietly. He had chosen to make the journey by sea, coming from the monastery of St Athan's in Glamorgan, a voyage of 50 miles or so. In those days it was possible to sail up to Caerwent from Portskewett (*Porth-is-y-coed* the harbour below the wood) via a tidal creek which today is but a trickly ditch, due largely to Brunel's upsetting the water table thereabouts when building the Severn Tunnel for the Great Western Railway. However, Tathan came by sea. On his arrival a stag trotted out of the nearby Wentwood and obligingly stood upon the mooring rope of the saint's boat to stop it drifting back to sea when the tide ebbed. Later on, when the monks felt hungry, it stretched out its neck and offered itself as a meal for them. The offer was promptly accepted. So here we have, in allegory if nothing else, Christianity superseding something pagan represented by a stag. What was this pagan belief?

Shakespeare, whose acquaintance with 'Other' shines through his artistic licence around life's spooky bits to an extent that must have disturbed his more inhibited Protestant contemporaries, puts a neat answer into the mouth of Mistress Page, one of 'The Merry Wives of Windsor'. She tells us: –

> "There is an old tale goes that Herne the hunter
> Sometime a keeper here in Windsor forest
> Doth all the winter-time, at still midnight,
> Walk round about an oak, with great ragg'd horns,
> And there he blasts the tree, and takes the cattle
> And makes milch-kine yield blood, and shakes a chain
> In a most hideous and dreadful manner."

We know that the name Herne is derived from the Celtic god Cernunnos. So let us examine him point by point as set out in Mistress Page's knowledgeable description.

"... the hunter ..." he is a nature god, his power manifested in the seasons, wildlife, and procreation.

"... all the winter-time ..." the Celts started their year on 1st November – Samain – by opening the gates of their underworld to let all ghouls and baleful spirits dwelling there rise to Earth and roam abroad through the cold and darkness of winter, no doubt spreading seasonal colds, coughs, blights, pestilence, and murrain far and wide as they went. As a Celtic god Cernunnos was no longer respectable by Shakespeare's day, so Mistress Page is happy to classify him with all the awful things which emerged at Hallowe'en, not to be sent back down below again until Beltane (May Day).

"... Walk round about an oak ..." An oak tree, presented to Shakespeare's audience as 'Herne's Oak', is necessary to the play's plot as a meeting place. However, at Rheims the remains of an altar to Cernunnos show him dispensing acorns (also described as 'coins' or 'grain') from a sack. Thus an oak in association with Cernunnos may serve to depict him as a bringer of seed, fertility, regeneration and strength. Neither forget that the oak is specifically linked with late Celtic religious practice, as Pliny points out in his description of Druidic ceremonies.

"with great ragg'd horns ..." Cernunnos is an antlered or horned god. He is well depicted on the Gundestrup cauldron, a darkly sombre and unsettling artefact. He also wears a neck-ring or 'torque'. As depicted in a sculpture found beneath Notre Dame Cathedral in Paris, he wears a torque on each horn, – rather fetchingly. We shall talk of torques later. Whether the horns of the aurochs or the antlers of a stag, they serve to emphasise his virile rutting nature.

His influence lingered well into the Middle Ages, too. Theodore of Tarsus, Archbishop of Canterbury (668 – 690) got very cross about the winter time habits of his flock and decreed, "If anyone at the kalends of January goes about as a stag or as a bull, making himself into a wild animal and dressing in the skin of a herd animal, and putting on the heads of beasts ... penance for three years, because this is devilish." Oh dear! But note the elements of winter and the turning of the the year,

Cernunnos – As depicted upon a panel of the Gundestrup Cauldron. Iron Age. Note two torques.

as well as the un-Christian 'something else' element in this mummery which so alarms Theodore ... whose life – if not his incumbency – must have overlapped that of Meurig, incidentally. Did anyone at Mathern collect a three-year penance?

Perhaps they did, or should have done, for even based upon what we know now, hi-jinks and dances involving someone dressed as an animal were widely spread. Summer still brings out the hobby horses at Minehead and Padstow. Throughout Wales the Mari Lwyd (grey Mary) a horse's skull carried upon a pole with a mechanism to allow its operator to gnash its teeth, and trailing yards of winding sheet behind it, turned up around Christmas and invaded houses known for supplies of food, drink, and welcoming good cheer. Its entry had first to be obtained by victory over the householders in a verse battle of wits through the barred door, however. Variations on this theme are many, and its revival in recent years has widened the jollifications still further. In the Cotswolds there is a tradition of caperings involving a bull's head, and at Abbot's Bromley in Staffordshire is found the most famous horn dance of all. In it six men dance with 'heads' of reindeer antlers on their shoulders, and a 'hunter' astride a hobby horse stalks them and twangs a bow. These days the dance is performed on the first Sunday after 4th September, but seventeenth century records place it at Christmas, New year, and Twelfth Night, – all winter and year's end appointments. The oldest antlers, now kept in the church, have been carbon dated to around AD1000. This is no charade invented for tourists; Cernunnos would recognise the form of his votaries.

"... and shakes a chain ..." Cernunnos, as upon the Gundestrup cauldron, sometimes carries a snake, in itself a symbol of rebirth in that it sheds its skin. Someone not knowing this but seeing a strangely depicted snake – on the Gundestrup cauldron it, too, seems to have horns – in a representation of the god might mistake it for the chain traditionally rattled by all ghosts and infernal spirits, even prior to Dickens carolling at Christmas. To Mistress Page and her gossips Cernunnos is a devil who blasts vegetation and causes death and sickness in cattle, – a complete reversal to his original ambitions around Mathern and elsewhere. We will leave the stag-drawn cart for a while. Let us turn our attention to the well.

Our first recorded reference to it is made by our old friend Nennius, of 'Great Heap' fame: "... There is a spring by the well of 'Pydew Meurig' (*Latin* Puteus = a well) and there is a log in the middle of the spring, and men may wash their hands and faces, and have the log under their feet when they wash. I have tested it and seen it myself. When the sea floods at high tide, the Severn spreads over the whole shore, and touches it, and reaches to the spring, and the spring is filled from the flood tide (which produces a Severn Bore of greater or lesser spectacle,ARU) it draws the log with it to the open sea (on the ebb tide ARU) and it is cast about in the sea for three days, but on the fourth day it is found in the same spring. Now it came to pass that a countryman buried it in the ground to test it, and on the fourth day it was found in the spring, and the countryman who took it and buried it died before the end of the month ..." This comes from Nennius' series on the 'Wonders of Britain'.

The Severn Estuary shore at Mathern is locally infamous for a particularly fine and clinging alluvial mud. Until Brunel ran his railway along the flat shoreline, the tides came inland for a mile or more. Before the Severn Bridge/M48 road was finished in 1966 it was possible for the water to come up to the mill at Mathern on very high tides. Old folk recall this (written 2018) and also St Pierre mansion (now a 'leisure resort') having its coal supply poled up Mounton Brook from the wharf at St Pierre Pill (again 'puteus', and applied both here in South Wales and across the Severn Sea in Somerset to a spring draining into a larger water course) in a barge c 1920.

In Nennius' day anyone ferried across or along the Severn Sea to Mathern would have landed on a mudbank as close as possible to what we now know as St. Tewdric's Well, "... a place near a meadow towards the Severn ..." as the Book of Llandaff has it. The traveller would then have needed to reach dry ground using whatever offered itself to assist him by way of a wooden jetty or causeway. At the worst he would have had to take off his breeks and stagger through the adhesive goo until he reached land firm enough to bear his weight, at which point a log in a spring-fed pool would have been the ideal place for him to stand whilst sluicing off the mud until, clean of leg once more, he could resume his trousers and proceed inland. No doubt a suitably basic wooden bowl or so was kept handy to aid such operations. If he also fastidiously washed his hands and face, his day's toilet was complete! Nennius has taken such pains, we note.

For the record, this well has never run dry in this author's experience, although it can be reduced to a leaf-mouldy sludge in ultra-heated droughts. Equally it does no more than surface-freeze thinly, probably wind-chilled, in the worst winter's weather, and is thus a reliable supply of water all year round. Almost certainly this is where "... a very clear fountain flowed, and the carriage was completely broken; he (Tewdric) then commended his spirit to God, and ordered the stags to depart; and having remained there alone, after a short space of time, he expired."

Just across the county border in Herefordshire there is another 'cart' story which parallels Tewdric's tale and is, according to a local historian the Rev'd. D.B. Gwilym-Jones, about a century older, c 485. It derives from the 'Book of Llandaff, too, and so presumably also has its origins in bardic tradition. One only hopes that the compilers of 'The Book of Llandaff' have not adjusted, over-sanitised, or otherwise edited the two tales to make them 'suitable' for a twelfth century Church book of record, and denied us something interesting about horned beasts, or people "... putting on the heads of horned beasts ..." in the process.

Rev'd Gwilym-Jones writes in his history of St. Clydawg's church in the village of Clodock, "... Clydawg the King or Ruler of Ewias was out hunting one day (according to the "Liber Landevensis/Book of Llandaff") and amongst those hunting with him was one who was jealous of his relationship with a lady friend. In his jealousy he killed Clydawg. On the day of his burial the two oxen pulling the cart, when they came to the ford across the river, [Monnow] refused to go across when the the yoke which joined them to the cart broke. He was buried, therefore, near the bank of the river. Such an act of murder made Clydawg, because of his godly life, a Martyr. For centuries afterwards he was known by the Celtic phrase, 'Methyr Clydawg' 'Martyr Clydawg' and an enclosure – Celtic 'Llan' – was created around his tomb and a Cell raised over his tomb."

On the opposite bank of the Monnow, downstream from the church and a hundred or so crow-flown yards from it, is St. Clydawg's well. It consists of a stone-lined basin fed by a small spring, and is covered by a stone slab about three feet in length and ten inches in width. This keeps out debris. Interestingly, its location is adjacent to the most feasible-looking place for wheeled traffic to ford the river, which runs in a wide trench it has cut for itself over the aeons through the local red sandstone, making its banks quite steep, angular, and rocky elsewhere in the vicinity. This circumstance would seem to confirm the intended fording place of Clydawg's collapsing cart to a nicety.

Further afield, St Gregory of Tours tells us about a curious French traffic accident of around AD 545 which has a similar ring to it. It centres around the daughter of King Theudebert, "... a great king, distinguished by every virtue ..." according to St Gregory, and Deuteria his queen, who seems to have been a serial adulteress with a penchant for collecting high-class husbands. St Gregory does not much approve of her. He writes, "... When Deuteria saw that her daughter was a grown-up woman, she was afraid that the king would desire her and take advantage of her. She put her in a cart drawn by untamed bulls (uncastrated, entire, ARU) and had her tipped over a bridge; she fell into the river and was drowned. This happened in the city of Verdun." We are luridly intrigued but cannot decipher what was really taking place in the Royal Family, or the municipality of Verdun, either. The sententious tones of Tacitus (c55 – c120) now echo in air.

In his 'Germania' he tells of the customs of several minor tribes, amongst whom he mentions the Anglii – Angles – as in Anglo-Saxon. From the second century onwards they were settling, by Roman army arrangements if nothing else, in the northern parts of Britannia. Perhaps some of their customs were sufficiently akin to those of the (furtive!) Britunculi for them to have felt readily at ease.

Tacitus writes, "... There is nothing particularly noteworthy about these people in detail, but they are distinguished by a common worship of Nerthus, or Mother Earth. They believe that she interests herself in human affairs and rides through their peoples. In an island of Ocean stands a sacred grove, and in that grove stands a car draped with a cloth which none but her priest may touch. The priest can feel the presence of the goddess in this holy of holies, and attends her, in deepest reverence, as her car is drawn by kine. Then follow days of rejoicing and merry-making in every place which she honours with her advent and stay. No one goes to war, no one takes up arms; every object of iron is locked away; then, and then only, are peace and quiet known and prized, until the goddess is again restored to her temple by the priest, when she has had her fill of the society of men. After that, the car, the cloth and, believe it if you will, the goddess herself are washed clean in a secluded lake. This service is performed by slaves who are immediately afterwards drowned in the lake. Thus the mystery begets terror and pious reluctance to ask what the sight can be that is allowed only to dying eyes."

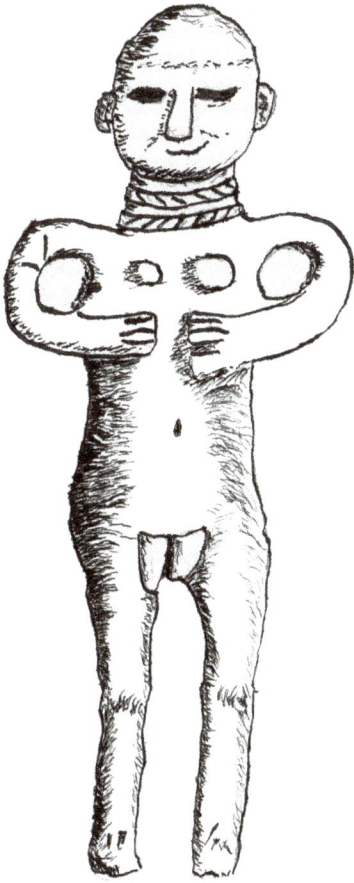

A late Bronze Age or Early Iron Age goddess, cast in bronze, from a bog at Vikso in Denmark. Note the two torques around her neck.

Archaeology, most notably in the bogs of Denmark, has found some statues assumed to be Nerthus. They are crudely shaped logs, worth hiding out of sight behind an awning over a cart. She also wears two neck rings – torques – just like Cernunnos. So, in combination, we have fertility deity, horned animals, torques, a cart, log statues, water, and violent or sudden death. But we have no common key, narrative, or tradition to understand these things properly, and may make what we will of them. There are human remains, too, the bog-acid 'tanned' skins of corpses from Danish bogs. We know them as Borre Fen man, Tollund man, Graubelle man, and a number of others. There were women, as well; – a decapitated girl from Roum, and a teenager from Windeby, who had been beaten up, blindfolded (or a very tight headband had slipped down) and then pinned beneath stakes in the bog waters to drown. The men all bore various mortal injuries, but the common factor was that they they had all been garrotted at some stage, – a rope substituting the torque, perhaps? So had a Mancunian, 'Pete Marsh', or Lindow Man as he is known to archaeology, (Lindow = *Llyn* a lake. *Du* black /dark). Discovered, like his Danish counterparts, in peat deposits, he had also had his throat cut, his his skull fractured, and – most likely – been stabbed in the chest. Maybe he was first knocked unconscious to render him oblivious to the rest. Who can say? Carbon dating assigns all these people to the late Iron Age/Roman times. The remains of highly decorated wagons have also been recovered from Dejbjerg in West Jutland. They had been carefully dismantled before being placed in the bogs. Why, we can only guess, but we note that both Clydawg's and Tewdric's carts had become unusable once they had reached water. The stomachs of some of the presumed sacrifices contained a vile porridge of just about every seed available for a Spring sowing or natural dissemination. Were they an offering to Nerthus? Goodness knows.

A later and lighter slant on this grim business is told us in a rather tongue-in-cheek story dating from eleventh century Norway, which had just become Christian under King Olaf Tryggvesson. A certain Gunnar Helming, spitefully accused of a murder someone else had committed, had hurriedly taken the scenic route to Sweden as a refugee, to wait there until his name was cleared at home. Skulking among the rustic Swedes, Gunnar found that they were keen on sacrificial celebrations and that the particular object of their worship was Frey, their nature god who rode upon a canopied wagon and was attended by a pretty young lady; – very Swedish! The peasants believed that the loggish Frey was indeed a living being and that he needed this lady's wifely company, for it was her duty to arrange all celebrations on his behalf, consulting with him beneath his canopy to ensure that everything went well. Gunnar approached the lady, assuming the role of a poor foreign traveller down on his luck and needing her aid. She consulted Frey and confirmed that Gunnar was indeed unlucky, because Frey did not view him favourably

The 'Dagenham Idol'. Iron Age; assumed to be a god.

at all. Unabashed, Gunnar responded that he would rather have her favour than Frey's any day. This presentation of his case appealed to the lady, at least, and since Gunnar was a cheery, ingenious and out-going sort of fellow, he contrived to become one of Frey's party. In due course the lady told him, "The people like you, so I think it will be best if you stay the winter and take part with me in the festivals when Frey ensures a fruitful year for the countryfolk. But Frey does not like you at all."

Frey's progress through the land continued, until on a long trail through the mountains they were engulfed by a terrific snow storm. Frey's local servants promptly headed for home, leaving the wagon, the lady, and Frey to fend for themselves. Gunnar took charge and led forward the horses carefully until, rather weary, he climbed into the driving seat. Frey's indignation drove him out again, and a fight started; all good Norse stories should have one. Gunnar was getting the worse of it until he called upon the aid of the new Christian God whom King Olaf had started to worship, whereupon the

Frey? An adapted tree branch from Broddenbjerg, Jutland. Iron Age.

'devil' who inhabited the image of Frey in the cart gave a shriek and fled into the storm. Gunnar then easily chopped up his log, just to make sure. The clouds parted, the sun shone, and Gunnar and the lady had a little talk. Her main problem was that she could no longer be Frey's priestess/bride if there was no Frey to attend. But the resourceful Gunnar was equal to the occasion. He simply put on Frey's clothing, and continued the tour in the god's guise. When they arrived at the next village on their route they found that the locals had arranged a great

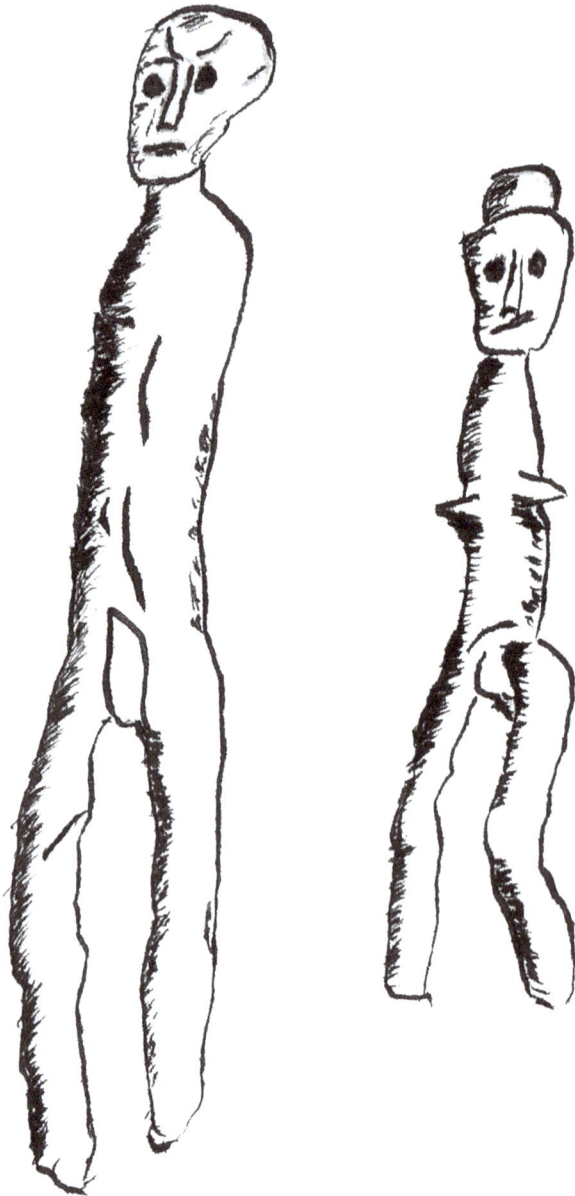

Frey and Freya? Adapted tree forks from Braak in Germany. Iron Age.

banquet for Frey. Gunnar was delighted, and so were the villagers, for they had seen the severity of the storm and were amazed that even Frey was able to take a wagon through the mountain passes and visit them in such weather. Further, 'Frey' thought so too and was able to speak of it whilst eating and drinking just like any good man, although he spoke little to anyone but his wife. They moved on from feast to feast, and as time passed it became rather obvious that Frey had worked his powers upon the land so well that even his wife was pregnant, a circumstance without precedent. Clearly they were all set for a fine and fruitful year. And so it proved. Gunnar's brother, Sigurd, contrived to get word to 'Frey' that the true murderer had been detected and dealt with, and that King Olaf was most eager to hear the amazing tales coming out of rural Sweden from Frey-Gunnar himself. 'Twas time to come home, therefore, and *de facto* Mr and Mrs Helming duly presented themselves before Olaf at Trondheim and, we may believe, lived happily ever after.

This lovely yarn, which we are not at all required to take too seriously, is about the last glimpse we have of folk memory founded around the cheerier elements of

An idol. Iron Age. Discovered near Teingrace.

what had been all too real in the pagan times of at least 800 years earlier. We only have the story because it tickled the Icelandic Statesman and historian Snorri Sturlusson (c1179 – 1241) enough for him to record it. Whilst based upon old traditions, it is doubtful that anyone's affairs had unfolded quite as narrated. It is a jibe at Swedish 'backwardness', in essence. We know that Frey had a sister, Freyja, who was equally Nature and Fertility personified as a god/goddess, and could be sister and/or wife to Frey as required. Perhaps some of the 'bog people' unearthed by archaeologists were Tacitus' slaves and were granted a period of high living as priest-husband or priestess-wife before being ritually killed and deposited in the bogs. The Celts certainly saw wells and springs as entrances to their under-world, and the curative properties of some springs have become the basis for spas which are still part of our own medical resources. To suggest that Tewdric and Clydawg officiated in some way from carts, subsequently dismantled, in a blessing-of-the-fields type of ceremony would not detract from their Christianity. They do not need to have been slain in this context and then have had their histories re-wrtitten to fit their 'images', as has been suggested occasionally. Over time the origins of a religious ceremony can separate entirely from its subsequent practice, – as is the case with the distribution of the Royal Maundy money, which at first sight has no connection with The Last Supper.

Yet there are still elements in Tewdric's tale which may give us pause for thought. If he was rendered comatose by a battle wound at Tintern, and was known to have wished for burial upon the Island of Echni, why was he subsequently jolted over the hills for six miles on an unsprung cart when the ebb and flow of a tide in the Wye and Severn estuary could have brought him to his chosen resting place? Could the well, described only as a washing place by Nennius the monk, have been held to have curative properties, natural or magical, and Tewdric have been brought to it in hope of a miracle?

Many churchyards have wells at or near their boundaries; Llangwm, Llangibby and Trellech come easily to mind, in addition to Mathern and Clodock. Very likely there are more, if searched out. Christianity's taking over earlier sacred sites is quite a common occurrence, advocated by Pope Gregory the Great, c540 – 604, when briefing St Augustine for his mission to England. He knew that people accustomed to worshipping in a particular locality would be all the happier to continue coming to it, and this might apply here. Tewdric's well itself lies in a little valley between his church and a mysterious rampart and ditch upon the opposite hill crest at Moyne's Court. This is a Jacobean house built upon the site of a little 13th century castle, now visible only in some foundations in the house's cellars. The ditch and rampart are the wrong way round for defensive purposes, the ditch being within the rampart, and so unlikely to have been associated with the castle. But they are quite in order for a sanctuary dating from the Neolithic age onwards. Until there is a proper archaeological investigation no date can be ascribed to them. But might Tewdric in his own day have inherited a traditional duty required of him in relation to an ancient sanctuary and the well? We do not know, so there we must leave it pending any factual evidence obtainable by the trowel.

It is Meurig, let us remember, with whom Nennius associates the well. Maybe something about Tewdric suggested caution to him, or maybe the grant of the 'Manor of Mathern' to the See of Llandaff by Meurig, a good 200 years before Nennius put quill to parchment, seemed to him a better piece of history to note for posterity. How can we judge, and do all parties justice?

Tewdric died as the result of a conflict in which he defended his people, the first duty of any ruler. If his Christianity was a little equivocal he was in good company. Raedwald, King of East Anglia, in his day 'Bretwalda' and Meurig's approximate contemporary, upset St Augustine's mission-aries by placing a crucifix amongst the other gods of his hall instead of clearing them away in favour of it. But he was clearly no fool, in the eyes of his contemporaries and ourselves. He was a great and pragmatic ruler, as history relates. Christianity offered him extra spiritual 'insur-ance' plus political status in the wider context of 'Romanitas' Europe, so he took it on board and so retained a credible political grip upon his neighbours, both Christian and pagan, keeping peace in the land in so far as its maintenance lay with him. Christian insights can be applied to earthly affairs without displaying garish labels; only good trees bear good fruit. Raedwald was such a tree. So, it appears, was Tewdric.

When later on we view the well-documented seventeenth century through the eyes of effective rulers, we shall be able better to discern the important priorities which imperfectly balance political life, vicious as our 'selfish genes'. In the end our Spiritual state conveys us from this world into Eternity as simple individuals, shorn of the transient earthly identities which are all that can be viewed subsequently by mortal historians. It is the overall quality of the choices we have made which defines us then.

Tewdric died around 595, give or take a decade, checking expansion by a body of early English. Let us conclude his story in the early Middle ages, by viewing the outline of Britain as it developed from the sixth century onward into better recorded times.

8

From 'Dark Ages' to 'Middle Ages'

Moving on from Roman times into the 'Dark Ages' we remarked that life became more lawless, individualistic, and shaped post c450 by immigrants who retained more of their own culture than would have been possible under the organised and regulated life of The Roman Empire. Yet the essentials of life still continued. There was not a sudden social collapse into a wilderness or a return to hunter-gatherer levels of civilisation. People remained people and made the best they could of circumstances, contributing to the common weal as need and inspiration suggested. Quite quickly, indeed, new forms of social organisation grew to accommodate the realities of the day.

To the West of the Fosse Way, roughly speaking, the stewards of the old Roman Imperial estates became rulers of 'Princedoms' and 'Kingdoms' in proportion to their resources, alliances, and their sheer ability to get their own way. A few years' lack of opposition from armed rivals, as chance may have had it in their localities, would no doubt have helped them in establishing their rule, too. People became used to a set pattern of life and, if it worked well for them, were all the more ready to support and defend it. It was a matter of self-interest, and their leaders in domestic affairs or in war took pains to give coherence to 'their' group of households. If they could enlarge the number of 'their' people by some means, such as marriage, affording protection, annexation, amalgamation or outright conquest, they would do so. Then the resources at their disposal became greater accordingly, and all those involved became stronger as a result. It was essentially safety in numbers, and a group identity with a common law code developed and confirmed this. They mostly spoke an ancient form of Welsh. King Tewdric fits well into this new and developing culture.

Eastward of the Fosse Way, again using this road as a dividing line, the post-Roman landscape was initially more fragmented. Amongst the farmsteads of indigenous Britons, wherever they were still identifiable as distinct groupings, were settlements of 'Saxons'. This name essentially meant 'Non-Latin-Speaker' to authors such as St Gildas and Nennius, who applied it to Anglo-Britons whose origins, often generations since, were Continental. They formed the armed and active sections of society which in time coalesced into larger units of population, native Britons included by absorption. Again, the principle was safety in numbers, living according to good law administered by their own Chieftains and Kings. When Bede relates the meeting between St Augustine and the Welsh bishops in 603 as having taken place upon the borders of the West Saxons and Hwicce (later Mercia), he is using in 'Hwicce' a name already out-of-date. He could have written Wessex (formerly Gewisse) and Mercia with equal truth, the earlier, smaller territories of Gewisse and Hwicce having been incorporated as elements of these greater powers some years previously. This was also true of a number of names which look quaint to us but may still be identified with parts of England, for example: – Wocensaetna, Lindisfarna mit Haethfeldande, Spalda, Cilternsaetna, Faerpinga, Cantwarena, and about two dozen others which flourished independently for a while and then combined with another group for greater strength.

In short, by 603 it is possible to speak accurately enough for our purposes of English (Anglo-Saxon) and Welsh kingdoms. The change from Roman polity had taken around 200 years to evolve thus far. But an overall concept of an English nation with political power residing in a single and undying Crown, regardless of the qualities of any particular monarch, was not to come about properly until after the tough and brutal imposition of the Norman system of feudal land tenure. This laid down systematically both the rights and obligations applicable to all classes of citizen, and was recorded plainly by the Domesday Book of 1086. Thereafter whoever wore The Crown was the empowered and legal Monarch of the whole land, not simply the individual who could inspire the greatest loyalty amongst the great landholders of the time, defend – with their help – the land from external aggression, give, and enforce by due fear and respect, good law within its borders, and enable all who dwelt in the land to feel safe and secure.

Until the Normans, however, such a settled state could disappear overnight with a King's death. For example, the Bretwalda King Edgar (reigned 959-975) was rowed upon the River Dee at Chester by other, lesser 'Kings' of territories within Britain who had endorsed his new Code of Laws. These stated in part, "... this [measure] is to be common to all the nation, whether Englishmen, Danes or Britons, in every province of my dominion ..." only to have this concept of dominion fall into pieces under Aethelred the Unready, reigned (978–1016). There was no accepted and imposed idea of 'dominion'; the character and ability of the King himself were all. It fell to the Danish King Canute to conquer and rule the land (1016-1035). He provided defence, good law and justice for the relief of his war-weary English subjects, and generally establish conditions in which they could prosper in peace and stability. Canute's nationality certainly grated somewhat with the old Anglo-Saxon aristocracy, but the nation welcomed the end which he provided to the former chaos and slaughter. William the Conqueror himself was a third generation 'Dane', whose family had compelled the French to give them land in France – ie 'Normandy', the territory of the Norsemen – in return for protection from other Vikings. It was William's adoption from the Franks of the concept of The Crown – sovereignty as a system – which made for stability and nationhood.

Why do such political developments of the eleventh century have any bearing upon our consideration of Tewdric, some 400 or so years earlier? They are valid because Tewdric drove back a 'Saxon' incursion. This was most probably a plundering/probing expedition by Angles from the still-forming English Kingdom of Mercia and, if it was fought around 595, it could be represented by Welsh chroniclers and bards as a Christian victory over pagans, for the Mercians at the time, especially under their formidable King Penda (reigned 632-654) were very pagan indeed. By checking Mercian expansion upon his eastern frontier, ill-defined though it may have been, Tewdric gave Meurig the breathing space to rule effectively for at least several decades and be given, long afterwards, the sobriquet 'Father of Wales'. The 'Book of Llandaff' tells us much upon which to elaborate.

The night before his battle at Tintern the Angel of the Lord tells Tewdric, "Go tomorrow to assist the people of God against the enemies of the Church of Christ … seeing thy face and knowing it they will, as usual, betake themselves to flight, and afterwards for the space of thirty years in the time of thy son, they will not dare to invade the country; and the natives and other inhabitants will be in quiet peace." There is plenty here worthy of closer attention.

For a start, Tewdric has won some earlier battles, because his enemies will run away "… as usual …" If this were not basically true, a bard's occasional-warrior audience jealous of its own prowess and hard-won fame would soon have corrected him, possibly by unpleasant means. Also an Angel of the Lord could not give a false prophecy, especially when the enemy is pagan; this much is dogma. So the Book's compilers and the bards' audiences must also have known, and agreed, that there had been about thirty years of peace and tranquillity in the land following the battle. If such a span of time, effectively a whole generation, were not an historical fact there would be no point in mentioning this prophecy in association with praise for a Christian King. Something in mighty Mercia took the pressure off Meurig for a good while, it seems. Meurig's own resources could never have driven back a full Mercian army. We must consider 'armies' shortly.

Then we have "… the natives and other inhabitants …" What might this mean? We know that at some point Meurig married Onbrawst, a princess from the Ircingafeld/Archenfield dominions which were broadly in present-day Hereforshire, perhaps echoed now by the village names of Aconbury and Arkstone. This is King Clydawg country, and borders the lands of the pagan Mercians who are the likeliest enemies in the story. By this marriage Meurig would have been an ally, if only in expectation, of the Ircingas. Could they have been the "… other inhabitants …" mentioned, annexed to Meurig's kingdom, but not yet assimilated in popular consciousness? Herefordshire was certainly English by Domesday Book times, so perhaps Ircingafeld came and went during the passage of the centuries? One thinks of Alsace – Lorraine and

Heligoland in more recent contexts. Can we ever know for certain? As an alternative, could a strong Meurig be sheltering a refugee population from a Welsh/British defeat somewhere fairly near at hand? We shall shortly mention the British collapse at Dyrrham Down in 577 as a possibility, but some particularly intense raiding from the Irish or water-borne Saxons landing in the West of Tewdric's domains might have had the same effect, even though we know nothing of any such event. The overall picture of Meurig's inheritance is far from bland, therefore. Let us try to look at the politics beyond his borders.

The main English powers close to Morgannwg (if it was so called in Tewdric's time) were Mercia to the north and east and, across the Severn Sea, Wessex to the south and west. Some authorities hold that present-day Worcestershire is in essence the land of the Hwicce. Be that as it may, Mercia stretched far to the east and north, and eventually contended with Northumbria for dominance in the land. Wessex also had great ambitions, and began expanding into the Midlands at the expense of some Kingdoms of Britons which still, during Tewdric's time, held lands in Gloucestershire and Oxfordshire, pinched between Mercia on their one side and Wessex on their other. The River Severn flows through Worcester, and continues seawards through Gloucester – (formerly Roman 'Glevum') – which was its lowest bridging point until the Severn Bridge of 1966. It splits present day Gloucestershire in two. Both Mercia and Wessex wanted to possess all its rich and fertile flood-plain. Inevitably there would be a clash between them. Crudely, this was the reality facing Tewdric and Meurig.

Wessex made the first move. In 577 the Anlgo-Saxon Chronicle states; "Cuthwine and Ceawlin fought with the Britons at a place called Deorham and killed three kings – Coinmail, Condidan, and Farinmail, and took three chesters – Gleawanceaster (Gloucester), Corinceaster (Cirencester), and Bathanceaster (Bath)." This engagement might well have sent a flood of refugees across the Severn estuary to seek shelter under King Tewdric in Morgannwg. Deorham, where Roman remains await detailed examination, is nowadays Dyrham, sheltering westwards of a steep scarp rising to around 60m/200ft, topped by rolling down-land and split by two distinct west-facing gullies. On a bluff there is a small Iron-age fort, and there is a much superior fortification at Little

Sodbury, about four miles northwards. Hereabouts an English force demolished a British alliance, much enlarging Anglo-Saxon England by way of result. Alas, we know nothing more about Cuthwine, Coinmail, Condidan, and Farinmail. Ceawlin alone has his moment of glory.

Walking over the parkland at Dyrham Park, now a late seventeenth century great house's domain, it is very easy to let one's imagination run riot in considering how Ceawlin and his forces could have dislodged a native army from what should have been a very good defensive position, obliging an attacker to charge uphill from nearly all directions. It would have been an infantry battle, and one starts mentally deploying troops in strong, self-sustaining units to manoeuvre, harass, and disorganise the defenders until a mutually supporting push overwhelms the Britons and they break ranks, which then fragment and flee in panic to be slaughtered piecemeal. Then one realises that a couple of thousand troops would be needed to produce this result. Reality dawns. Tewdric at Tintern probably had fewer than 200 men to deny the passage of the ford. Allow the, conjectured, Mercians a similar number – or fewer if just a plundering/scouting force – and between 300 and 400 at the most would have been engaged overall. The same applies at Dyrham. Compared with the well organised 'fyrd' military system of King Alfred the Great (ruled 871-900) the forces which clashed at Dyrham in 577 were bands of largely civilian fighters with a few professional warriors around their leaders. Let us be generous and say around 700 overall fought that day.

We know we are fairly safe in making such a statement because of the Law Code of 694 which was laid down by one of King Ceawlin's successors in Wessex, King Ine, (reigned 688-926). He sets out clearly how groups of men should be classified:-

"Up to 7men = Thieves
7 – 35 men = Raiders or a band
36 or more men = a 'here', ie an army"

This can be borne out by archaeology. The Sutton Hoo ship, which was old, somewhat repaired, and redundant (or for ceremonial use only?) when it was buried, was of late 6th century construction. It has oar pins for 36 rowers. The long ships that the Vikings used when raiding from the late 8th century onwards are reckoned to have been capable of carrying 50 armed men with ease, if lack of comfort. The Gokstad ship, replicas of which have sailed the Atlantic, has oar-slots for 32 rowers, and in recent years Danish shipwrights have replicated many of the splendid Roskilde Fjord Viking-era boats. These have been thoroughly tested, and with crews of around 50 young and able personnel have been found very sea-worthy. They have surprised archaeologists by both their speed, an average of 10 knots in good conditions, and manoeuvrability. For a static rural community suddenly to have two or more of these, all carrying 50 young, fit, well-armed and motivated Englishmen descend on it out of the blue, and then go to work slaughtering all who resisted them and their desires, was beyond the capacity of any localised home guard to check.

Nor, for that matter, did all 'Saxon invaders' necessarily come from 'over there' in Continental Europe. Some sons and grandsons of long-settled English in the eastern shires could occasionally have launched ships from estuaries, creeks, and harbours near their family farms, and set out a-pirating. Such activity was Carausius' excuse and St. Gildas' nightmare. The Channel and north coast of Gaul were favourite pirate prospecting places, but the western British kingdoms from 500 or so were also worth their attention to try their luck, raiding for ready cash and tradeable goods, such as concubines and slaves, or even with settlement in view if circumstances seemed in their dominating favour. In such a case some of their descendants could have fought for their land-holdings, so acquired, along with the British kings at Dyrham, and later that day found themselves subjects of English royalty once again. We cannot say with certainty. Battles were fought throughout this time by lords for self-interest, not from any racial or idealogical motives. Nor were they even dressed up in such parlance, beyond the sort of 'Churchy' utterances with which later historians graced the Book of Llandaff.

When Meurig ruled in 'Wales', this was the picture in England, – Saxon Kingdoms striving for riches, land, dominance and glory. Their interest lay where these were readily to be obtained, whilst putting serious rivals out of contention. Small Welsh Kingdoms could wait.

Wherever there were lands into which to expand, the main players could collect new assets. Thus Ceawlin had been successful against King Ethelbert of Kent, driving him back in 568 from the area now known as Hampshire, into his Kentish peninsular where he had only the trading wealth of the 'Saxons' across the sea to draw upon. However, Ceawlin had over-reached himself at Dyrham, and also had domestic problems in his own lands, for we read of him in the Anglo-Saxon Chronicle, "584 – In this year Ceawlin and Cutha fought the Britons in the place called Fethan Leag, and Cutha was killed. Ceawlin took many towns and innumerable spoils of war, and returned in wrath to his own country," And in 592 – "Ceawlin was driven out of the Vale of Pewsey." Then in 593 – "In this year died Ceawlin. And Cwichelm and Crida." We recall, also, that by 597 Ethelbert of Kent is 'Bretwalda', the unassailable-amongst-equals of his contemporary Anglo-Saxon Kings. He cannily welcomed St Augustine, was converted (to some extent) to Christianity, and was able to guarantee Augustine a safe passage to the southern shores of The Severn Sea, traditionally at Aust on the boundary of the Hwicce and Gewisse in 603 to confer with the Welsh Bishops. Ethelbert has recovered splendidly. Ceawlin is no more. Who is in the wings awaiting his time and chance? Meurig, being a sensible fellow, would have pondered this question.

He would, if old enough in 584 to understand the talk of his elders, have grasped that if Ceawlin had taken, ". . . many towns and innumerable spoils of war . . ." at Fethan Leag, yet returned, ". . . in wrath to his own country . . ." he had not gone home quite as contented as might have been expected. He was somehow in difficulties. For the record, Fethan Leag is reckoned to be the little village of Stoke Lyne in rural north Oxfordshire, a pleasant place where the older buildings are constructed of a local, pale amber-coloured stone which gives them the appearance of having been built of ginger biscuits. The witch's house in the Hansel and Gretel story comes to mind! The village lies right upon the Mercian frontier of Ceawlin's day, and it may be that he found himself fighting Mercians, not Britons, and got the worse of it in that locality at least. Add to that a usurpation of the Wessex kingship by one Ceol, and it is clear that Ceawlin was a spent force after 584. Perhaps Mercian probing to discover just what lay south of its flexible bounds led directly to Tewdric's battle at Tintern a few years later. Wessex was definitely expelled from 'Premier League' Anglo-Saxon politics in the region in 628, according to the Anglo-Saxon Chronicle, when "... Cynegils and Cwichelm (of Wessex) fought with Penda (of Mercia) at Cirencester, and came to an agreement with him." In simple terms Mercia took Cirencester, and by implication Gloucester, away from Wessex, and Penda married Cynegil's daughter, Cynwise, as part of the peace settlement. And Penda was not even a king at the time, just an ambitious lord.

If Penda then held the bridge at Gloucester he could have moved along the Severn and through the Forest of Dean, much larger then than now, to menace Meurig. But there were bigger moves afoot in England. In 600 Aethelfrith of Northumbria cleared the British away from his route northwards to Scotland at Caertref/Catterick, a battle celebrated by the bard Aneurin in his poem about the 'Goddothin' nation (known to the Romans as the *Vottadini* and associated with both Strathclyde and Gwynedd). Aneurin names the heroes and tells how wonderfully arrayed they all were, and how sumptuously they had feasted and drunk before the battle. The poem may be read as a cautionary tale against going off to fight whilst suffering from a hang-over. Aethelfrith could then expand his territory northwards, gather 'spoils' and plunder with which to enrich himself and his followers, and recruit un-attached warriors to his court with expectations of lasting praise, fame, rewards of gold, weapons, armour, horses, slaves (wenches), and grants of land, all after the campaign in hand had gone well through their efforts. And assuming that they had survived it, of course.

This was the system, but it relied on having fresh and rich lands to conquer on at least one of a king's frontiers. Essex. Sussex, Kent, East Anglia, and even Wessex to an extent, were not in that happy position. No early English King was ever praised by bards and given glory and immortal renown for settling merchants in his realm, and taxing them but moderately for his personal and court's income. Fame, a lasting reputation, and get-rich-quick wealth were for successful warrior heroes only. This was Meurig's problem if he ever harboured military ambitions, but we may assume that merchants came to his realm's long coastline well before the Old English name 'Chepstow' appeared in any documents. Meurig and his lands could certainly have prospered if he had remained unmolested by vastly superior forces during the early 600s.

After success at Catterick, Aethelfrith predictably moved northwards and attacked the Scots successfully at Degestan in 603. He would not lack for fighting men thereafter. In 624/'25 Raedwald of East Anglia helped a temporarily exiled Edwin of Northumbria regain his throne. Terrific upheavals followed in 625/'26 as Cwichelm of Wessex sent an almost-successful assassin to murder Edwin, who retaliated by marching an army from Northumbria to Wessex and ravaging the land almost unopposed. In other words, compared with the now elderly Cwichelm, Edwin had the larger number of career warriors, battle-toughened and keen on pillaging treasure from Wessex. Since they were successful, even more of their type would seek out employment with Edwin, who did nothing to try and mediate between Penda and Cwichelm over Cirencester in 628. Had he been able, or taken the trouble, to do so he would have kept Penda bothered with the potentially hostile power of Wessex on his southern frontier to guard against, thus leaving fewer troops available to him to permit new Mercian aggression in the North. For whatever reasons Edwin did not/could not do this, and so was defeated in 632 at Hatfield near Doncaster after Penda had made a temporary alliance with the Welsh King Cadwallon of Gwynedd to guarantee a numerical superiority, one supposes, over Edwin before attacking him. Cadwallon at that time would have had some kingly influence stretching from Anglesey to Strathclyde, the west of the Pennines being then still British. But he would have done well to have heeded wisdom relating to the use of long spoons when supping with devils. He was casually thrown over by Penda and slaughtered in 634 when a son of Aethelfrith, Oswald, obtained the Northumbrian crown, turned on Penda successfully, and ruled until 642 when Penda had his revenge by defeating and killing him in battle. Penda continued as a constant threat in the land until he died in the slaughter whilst fighting King Oswy of Northumbria in 654.

This digression into the murky world of heroic warrior early English politics will serve to show how the thirty years of peace granted to Meurig very probably came about because, although he obviously stood in the path of his powerful neighbours if they had had any territorial ambitions concerning Wales, they were too busy fighting each other to bother much about him. It helps us give him a plausible dating for his reign, too, for Mercia in particular would not have wanted the running sore of troublesome Welshmen forever destabilising its land frontier with Wales by pin-prick raids, incursions, and little local wars which might have allowed any English lordly usurpers to emulate the causes of Ceawlin's downfall. So a peacefully inclined Meurig suited Penda's northern designs wonderfully. However, it was just as well for Meurig that Penda never succeeded in annexing Northumbria, and then looked around for some more territory into which to expand as profitably as possible.

This brings our tale of Saint and King Tewdric and King Meurig ap Tewdric well into the seventh century. If our conjectures are roughly right, it backs up the bards' lays and the Book of Llandaff in adequate measure. We could leave it there, with a suitable 'REQUIESCANT IN PACE'.

Yet there is more to come. This author, chancing one fine day to be in St Tewdric's church and telling Tewdric's Tale to a most attentive visitor, found himself being interrogated in turn with some very sensible and penetrating questions. The visitor was most pleased to climb the 89 uneven and downright eccentric steps of the 1480 church tower, and view the landscape from the top of it (all H&S issues fully accepted as the visitor's own responsibility. The tower is not known to have killed or injured anyone during the 539 or so years it has stood, but the virus of No-Win=No-Fee lawyers has turned too many of us into acquisitive, perjuring, spineless dolts devoid of common sense, so a little speech nowadays has to be made – preferably before an independent witness – if anyone wants to climb it.) From its top St Pierre Pill may be admired in context, cf Nennius and The Well; the Bishop's Palace next door, gazed upon; and a whole vista of history demonstrated epoch by epoch. For the next half hour or so we did this, and conjectured upon the possibilities of smuggling goods and people successfully to land from the Pill. These days they are very good indeed, the Welsh Coastal Footpath drawing inland those who might arrive without maps. The path readily shows how to reach the A 48 road, with its useful 'bus services, mostly by footpath and byway. The visitor seemed both impressed and rather thoughtful, and handed over his card as we parted. It went into a shirt pocket unread, and was later discovered there by this author's wife doing a routine and careful check for what might otherwise end up in her washing machine.

It read; "Maurice Whitehead, Professor of History, Associate Dean (*Bologna*) Postgraduate Research Facility, Swansea University". Subsequent contact revealed . . .

"Tewdric; the Opera"

Let us continue for a few more chapters.

9

Tewdric – the Opera, "Sanctus Tewdricus sive Pastor Bonus"

The Millennium brought with it all sorts of celebrations, events, and amazements, and our local Saint suddenly became the focus of musical research. This derived, not from 'Covent Garden', 'La Scala', nor 'The Met', but from Dr. Peter Leech, conductor and musicologist, browsing in a little old shop in London. From this slightly Dickensian beginning it proceeded, not to rehearsal rooms, nor to recording studios, but to quiet archives in still places where written records slumber awaiting the rekindling of fires long grown cold and ashy. To set the scene, let us unfold the 'Tale of Tewdric', now "Sanctus Tewdricus sive Pastor Bonus" (*St Tewdric or The Good shepherd"* – cf St John's Gospel 10. 11) as told in a rather startling synopsis with a cast of characters hitherto un-guessed at: –

"The action opens in the camp of the Welsh army where Mauricus reads a letter informing him that a Saxon attack is imminent and that his younger brother, Arthurus (who is not mentioned by the Llandaff chronicler. ARU) has joined the ranks of the enemy. Mauricus agonizes over Arthurus' defection and eventually decides to abdicate in his brother's favour in order to spare his homeland from the ravages of war. Malcolmus encourages the prince to resist, reminding him of the injuries his people and his hermit father would suffer under the godless Saxons. Mauricus agrees to send Malcolmus to his brother incognito in order to negotiate a settlement; meanwhile, he will summon the troops to fight if necessary.

"The second scene is set in the Saxon camp, where Sigertus, Fridericus, and Otho boast of their victories over the Christians. Athurus is horrified when the three warlords begin stabbing a crucifix that they have hurled to the ground. Sigertus mocks Arthurus' futile protests and, when the prince tries to dissuade them them from their sacrilege, he stabs Arturus in the hands.

"In scene three, Arthurus' companion Ulfadus comes to summon him to battle against his kinsmen. Arthurus swears vengeance against Fridericus and convinces Ulfadus to go to the Welsh camp and beg for forgiveness.

"Tewdricus' hermitage is the setting for scene four. The Angel of the Forest calls upon the reluctant Saint to leave the beauty and silence of the woods for the turmoil and agony of the battle field. The Guardian Angel of Britain announces that the trees will soon confirm the divine decree, and the Angel of the Forest promises to become invisible and follow the saint to war. Tewdricus hesitates until the green leaves of a nearby oak suddenly wither and a laurel branch is miraculously transformed into a crown. Music fills the air as Tewdricus takes up his armour.

"The scene shifts to the battlefield, where Malcolmus, who has failed to reach the Saxon camp, wanders in aimless panic. The Angel of Britain announces that the Welsh army has been routed and that Mauricus is prepared to surrender to the usurpers. Malcolmus casts aside his shield and helmet in despair. When Ulfadus appears, Malcomus expects to be killed. Instead, Ulfadus reports that Arturus has renounced his allegiance to the Saxons and wishes to return home.

"The sixth scene finds Fridericus in pursuit of Mauricus. Ulfadus returns from the rout, and encourages Arthurus with the news that his brother still lives. Arthurus beheads Fridericus, puts the gory trophy and the fallen crucifix in a bag, and prepares to flee the Saxon camp.

"In scene seven, Arthurus, Mauricus, and Tewdricus meet by chance in the woods. After a tearful reunion, the saint inspires his sons to launch a counter-attack. In the Saxon camp, Sigertus and Otho swear to commemorate the death of Fridericus by massacring the Welsh.

After their exit, the Angel of Britain describes the off-stage battle. He announces that Mauricus leads the Welsh to victory, whilst Arthurus expiates his guilt with his sword.

"In the closing scene, Malcolmus again meets Ulfadus on the battlefield. Fearing that Ulfadus will trick him to escape capture by the Welsh, the cowardly Malcolmus kills his erstwhile friend. Sigertus surrenders to Tewdricus. Arthurus urges that the defeated king be put to death, but Tewdricus orders that he be spared. The treacherous Saxon stabs Arthurus, and Tewdricus dies of wounds he has suffered in the battle."

(This account was re-discovered in the archives of the Cheshire Record Office, where it is catalogued as Crewe Cowper Collection, ref DCC13.)

Having become accustomed to the 'Book of Llandaff' for a source, this wild and gory story is a surprise indeed. That it owes something to 'The Book of Llandaff' is undeniable, but along with it we find another source which is likewise worth giving in full before revealing the all-important context of our opera. This version comes from one John Wilson's "The English Martyrologe . . . a summary of the most renowned and illustrious Saints of the three Kingdoms – England, Scotland and Ireland." First published in 1608, its 1672 edition refers to Tewdric thus:-

"At Mathern in Clamorganshire of Wales, in the Diocesse of Landaffe, the Commemoration of S. Theoderick King of Clamorgan, and Martyr, who leaving the care of his Kingdome to his son Mauricke, became an Ermite, leading a strict kind of Monasticall life, until the Saxons invading that Province, he was by his subjects drawn out into the field by force against them whom he victoriously overthrew and chased away; but being deadly wounded in the battaile, and hastening home to his Hermitage, he dyed in the way at the foresaid place of Mathern, where his son Maurick built a goodly Church in his honour, and placed his holy body there, which was in great veneration of all the Country round about, even until this last age, when the Bishop of Llandaffe found the same whole and incorrupt, after a thousand years it had lain there, with the mark of his deadly wound remaining still in his skull. He is called in the British tongue Tewdrick, and suffered about the year of Christ, five hundred and forty."

Both the above accounts of Tewdric's victory over the 'Saxons' are post-Reformation in origin. The first is the outline of a drama, which had musical interludes added subsequently (so making it an opera) written and performed by students at the Jesuit College founded in 1593 by Fr Robert Persons SJ (1546 – 1610) at St. Omers in the Low Countries. Fr Persons is often bracketed in English history textbooks with Fr Edmund Campion SJ, whom he joined in a dangerous mission in England and Wales. Its aim was to render foreign support and encouragement to Roman Catholic recusants, who followed the old faith as opposed to the official Protestantism of the Elizabethan State, and who accordingly were obliged as a matter of conscience to decide between obeying their chosen belief and manner of worship, or conforming with the laws of the land.

The recusants' uncomfortable personal situation had been made downright dangerous by a blunder on the part of Pope Pius V, who in 1570 issued a papal bull – 'Regnans in Excelsis' – which at a stroke excommunicated Queen Elizabeth I and absolved her subjects from any allegiance to her and her government. In terms of conscience, therefore, all who obeyed Elizabeth were spiritual traitors to the Pope, officially 'Christ's Vicar upon Earth', and stood therefore in peril of eternal damnation. Conversely, if they were disloyal to Queen and Country in obedience to Pope Pius, the ghastly fate of hanging-drawing-and-quartering awaited them as traitors to the Crown by due process of English law. Fr Campion, indeed, was captured, tried and suffered such an execution as being a subversive and a foreign agent. So far as we can now ascertain, the great majority of Elizabeth's Roman Catholic subjects simply wanted to be left alone to worship in their preferred style. But the treasonable potential for *carte blanche* terrorism sanctioned by Pope Pius gave a self-perceived licence to ambitious hot-head bigots to act as they wished in pursuit of their aims, be these vaunted at some stage as religious, political, or both.

Therefore the authorities were obliged to act to counter every hint of treason. It was all a terrible under-current in the land, quite out of proportion to any hostile intentions by the general law-abiding majority of Roman Catholics, who automatically came to be regarded as untrustworthy and potentially murderous. The problem persisted, and fed upon itself. It produced a number of half-baked plots by vain-glorious zealots, culminating in the politically unavoidable execution of the Roman Catholic Mary Queen of Scots in 1587, even as the Spanish Armada was busily assembling to sail the following year in an attempt to 're-convert' England by force of arms. Mary was a direct descendant of Henry VII, and so stood as the legitimate successor to The Throne should Elizabeth die without an heir. The associated politics, both domestic and international, of this era would fill a bulky book. For present purposes it is sufficient for us to appreciate that by this time Roman Catholics were, unsurprisingly, suspected as being potentially hostile to Queen and country.

Elizabeth herself had been obliged several times to change her religious complexion during the course of her early life; from Roman Catholic – but with spiritual allegiance owed to her father Henry VIII as self-proclaimed Head of the Church in England, and not to the (Borgia) Pope Alexander VI; to ideological Protestant under the rule of her half-brother Edward VI; to full-blown Roman Catholic once more when her half-sister (Bloody) Mary I came to the throne. Next she found herself Queen in her own right, and in the same position as Head of the Church in England as her father. She said plainly, "I would not have windows into men's souls," and in dealing with the perennial controversy over the nature of the Sacrament of the Mass, used as a litmus test of Protestant or Roman Catholic belief, she resorted to verse; "'Twas God the Word that spake it, / He took the Bread and brake it; / And what the word did make it; / That I believe and take it." We shall never know for certain her true beliefs. Rulers are as constrained by events as engaged in governing them. So it was with Good Queen Bess. And her realm enjoyed peace and her people prospered.

The fact remains, however, that throughout the sixteenth and seventeenth centuries, and indeed beyond, a considerable number of people preferred the old style of worship. Whilst outwardly conforming to the Protestant rites required by the government of the day, they took their personal spiritual comfort from the old Roman Catholic forms. To encourage and minister to them an 'underground' network of priests, usually Jesuits, was organised, and something of a cloak-and-dagger traffic in personnel and materials supported it.

A busy little port like Chepstow had proper arrangements for obtaining customs revenues from certain classes of goods, so Bibles which turned out to be written in Latin or were not quite the Authorized Version when read, and clerical vestments of an unusual cloth and cut, would have attracted notice if arriving there by boat in any quantity. But a quiet creek like St Pierre Pill was a different matter. Further, the minor gentry of the area had a sympathy with the old worship, which was maintained at the level of family connections amongst the manors and farms, diffusing guardedly inland through Welsh-speaking Wales and into the midland English shires.

A particular safe haven for Jesuit activity was The Cwm farm in the valley of the River Monnow, situated in the quiet hills north-east of the gentrified Raglan Castle, in Elizabeth's time the seat of the fourth Earl of Worcester, himself a Roman Catholic and one of the Queen's favourites at court. She remarked of him that he ". . . reconciled what she believed impossible, a stiff papist to a good subject . . ." She appointed him her Master of the Horse, the senior personal attendant to the Sovereign upon all state occasions when horses are employed. Although the Earl served as Earl Marshal at the coronation of James I in 1603, and was Lord Great Chamberlain to Charles I, he was still subject to all the restrictions, fines, and petty annoyances of the times because of his non-conformity to the required formal professions of Protestantism. Personally, he worshipped as he chose and served his monarchs well and faithfully. This was all that Elizabeth wanted to ask of her people. All adapted themselves to it, apart from the inevitable zealot bigots whose activities fouled the atmosphere for everyone indiscriminately.

However, since most others of the Earl's persuasion lacked his vast wealth and resources, and had to live day-to-day life as it affected them in the wider community, they necessarily maintained a spiritual life on two levels and paid lip-service, tithes, and formal observance to the Protestant Church as the law required. They then made their private devotions in small 'house congregations' where Divine Service was conducted in secret by a Roman Catholic priest. Very likely such priests were Jesuits travelling through the land *incognito,* taking on the identities of family relatives, or tutors to the children of the wealthier households. Certainly this double-outlook in religious matters was widely appreciated, understood, passively supported, and winked at by the local authorities. It served its spiritual purpose, and would not have endured for more than a couple of months if any attempt had been made to put an end to it – as events in 1679 were to demonstrate.

The era we are considering here is the late sixteenth century, essentially the time of Bishop Francis Godwin who, in the words of John Wilson's 'English Martyrologie' (quoted above) found Tewdric's corpse "... whole and incorrupt after a thousand years it had lain there ..." But this is not exactly what Bishop Godwin reported, as we have seen. The miraculous, appropriate to the status of a saint, is creeping into the record written for Roman Catholic eyes in exile upon the Continent and for students obtaining the finer points of their religious education at the Jesuit St Omers College. It is here that the 'opera' of Tewdric came into being. It could have been written as an instructional drama demonstrating the Christian virtues of love and forgiveness but, in addition, it is just as plausibly a comment upon the political outrages against justice in the events of 1679. We shall deal with these matters in the next chapter.

What is not disputed is that a small and regular traffic of personnel and materials to support Roman Catholic worship in Wales passed through such points of entry as St Pierre Pill, and were conveyed onwards to the wider community of safe houses by a basically law-abiding population applying compassion and common sense to matters which it judged no-one's business but their own. For their own safety and the prevention of embarrassment to themselves and their families, not to mention social connections upon their return from St Omers, the young students directly involved adopted aliases both when at the college and when on their travels. Diligent work by Prof. Whitehead and Dr. Leech has identified the likeliest contenders for the opera's authorship. All of them were students at St Omers around 1679, and some of them became embroiled in the politics of that era, risking imprisonment and death for their faith. These days we would term their alleged wrongs 'ideological' and their treatment at law unjust. For all the difference their presence amongst the Welsh farmers and minor gentry made to anything of legal or administrative substance, they might just as well have been left alone.

But there was political conflict in London, and an easily grasped 'black' versus 'white' interpretation of the issues exemplified by Tewdric's battle and death, as conceived by fertile and ambitious young minds, was ideal teaching material for the St Omers Jesuits. It is very interesting that a thousand year old tradition of martyrdom in the course of winning victory over the enemies of the Christian Faith came readily to mind amongst the Welsh St Omers' students. Tewdric must have been better remembered then than he is nowadays: he was part of the cultural environment. Divine intervention by Angels is common both to the 'Book of Llandaff' and to the 'opera'. And an underlying belief in justice and righteousness beyond the expediencies of this material world resonates powerfully with the human psyche, unless this be so warped by some narrow selfish ideology that all compassion and generosity have vanished into a psychopathic limbo. Music is a deeply felt and universal language which, in ways not at all well understood, evokes a response directly from the unconscious mind – or, at any rate, for those who will allow mind to exist with independence from brain. It is from the later scenes of the Opera that its music has come down to us, thanks to a chance discovery in London by Dr. Leech which set him upon the main trail of the work. The piece, let it be stated, is written entirely in Latin – the language of learning and culture which endured far beyond the seventeenth century – and its musical notation is of an uncommon kind even for the period. Yet, the opera 'speaks', and there may yet be more to emerge from the archives. All honour to the scholarship which has found it.

We must now turn to the grim events which provided the background to its seventeenth century production.

10

Politics Most Foul

We have noted how Roman Catholics wishing to worship after their own fashion could easily be suspected of being traitors and potential murderers of all who did not share their religious views. Nor was such suspicion allayed by those among them who had embraced the Papal Curia approved practice of 'equivocation'. In essence this meant keeping one's true religious preference secret, save to God, and uttering whatever outright lies upon the subject might keep one out of trouble with the secular authorities. It was promoted by the Jesuits, especially, as a means of personal safety both in Eternity and in the here-and-now, but also had the obvious if unintended side-effect of implying that nothing spoken by a recusant could be relied upon.

"Faith! Here's an equivocator," chortles Macbeth's bored and tipsy porter, pretending to guard the gates of Hell, "that could swear in both the scales against either scale; who committed treason enough for God's sake, yet could not equivocate to Heaven! O! Come *in,* equivocator!" And no doubt Shakespeare's audience laughed, be their mirth a little uneasy. Perhaps some fellow standing alongside them in the theatre's pit was a Roman Catholic who had a dagger under his doublet, and just might start slaying all within reach upon some secret signal ... From either pan of the divine scales he could swear against the other with a clear conscience, for so said his Pope. And who could suggest how many of him there might be, moreover?

So suspicion nagged away at the back of everyone's mind, although the 'Keep calm and carry on' outlook of some centuries thereafter prevailed overall. As the sixteenth century slid into the seventeenth there were anxiety and unease enough to occupy minds in any case. Good

Queen Bess died in 1603. James I (and VI of Scotland, Mary Queen of Scots' son) succeeded her. 1605, Roman Catholic Guy Fawkes tried to blow him up along with his Parliament. James was not fond of Parliaments and was apt to do without them as much as possible, which gave men of substance in his realm little cause to feel that their views were being heeded in its governance. Under his son Charles I their discontent about this and other matters erupted into civil war in 1642, sputtering on till 1651, three years after Charles' head had rolled before the executioner's axe. A commercial war with the Dutch broke out 1651–57, Protestant Oliver Cromwell actually allying England with Roman Catholic France, and sending troops to the Low Countries to aid the French against the Dutch forces. 'Protector' Oliver Cromwell died in 1658, but his military dictatorship continued. A fully lawless rule by the soldiery was ended in 1660, when Charles II returned from exile to general relief and acclaim. Plague decimated London in 1665. Another war against the Dutch was launched, ending disastrously in 1667. In1666 the Great Fire of London obliterated much of the capital. A new alliance with the French (under the 'Sun King', Louis XIV) was negotiated in 1670. A further war against the Dutch followed in 1672, and was quickly concluded following Parliamentary outrage. Louis XIV was rumoured (correctly) to be paying Charles II huge sums to enable him to by-pass Parliament for his expenditure. Further rumour (likewise true) circulated that a secret clause in the Louis XIV 1670 treaty required Charles to return England to Roman Catholic worship. Charles' brother Prince James Duke of York, later James II, was openly Roman Catholic … It was clear that government was not as transparent and non-corrupt as it might have been. Thoughtful folk muttered together, wondering what would happen next.

In short, there was plenty in the air to make a straightforward Protestant Englishman feel uneasy. From as far back as Magna Carta in 1215 an English king was not above his own laws. Initially this had meant that his lords had wanted a practical share in how the country was governed, but on the Continent such restraints upon royal power had not developed. Charles I had tried to base his rule upon the 'The Divine Right of Kings', the idea enshrined in the Biblical justification of kings being appointed by God and therefore accountable to none but God, both in matters of State and of that State's Religion. This system was alien to the English way of proceeding, Parliament even having a say in Elizabeth's day, albeit very limited, on how taxes were raised and spent, and in how laws were made and enforced. By contrast, when Louis XIV assumed the French throne in 1643 he was able at the age of 17 (in 1655) to remark quite casually, "L' Etat, c'est moi," ("I alone comprise the State") and mean it. Further, he could back up this claim by force of arms, and occasionally did so. There were no 'ancient liberties' of a vaguely Magna Carta kind for the French. Louis reckoned himself divinely appointed, he was supported by a financially privileged Roman Catholic Church, and any who doubted, let alone opposed him, simply vanished from the scene. (Such governments are not unknown around the world today, of course.) When in 1660 "The King Enjoyed his Own Again" as Charles II formally ascended the Throne, Englishmen had had a taste of government-by-non-accountable-force, having just fought a civil war to prevent it and then finding themselves under the Puritan rule of Cromwell, followed by The Major Generals. They had not been impressed by such an outcome. Its similarity with the French system was seen, correctly, as tyranny. Protestant Englishmen did not want a Divine Right style of government ruling them; Cromwell's all-pervading enforced Puritanism had been bad enough.

Therefore, prospering post 1660 in a State ruled by laws overseen and enforced by a Parliament chosen by 'the better sort', though without regular elections, Englishmen suspected that honest governance acceptable to them was not quite what was taking place. Were there Roman Catholics influencing Crown and Council against the interests of good, honest, hard-working Protestants? How might these Papists subvert the 'common weal'? How many such 'traitors' might there really be? Where were they? Did they hold positions of power as magistrates, army officers, naval commanders, members of Parliament, personnel of the King's Privy Council, even? What if over half the country were really Roman Catholic, equivocating as necessary? What if they all suddenly appeared in arms and took over the government? Was anyone safe any more? Were law and liberty about to be horribly overthrown? Was the government one huge deceit of the people? In fact, who could be trusted? Was another civil war about to break out along religious lines?

In this way a general, low-pitched, formless distrust of Authority pervaded all levels of society. It needed but a spark for panic to ensue. And, as is typical when trust between Government and the governed breaks down, this came from just the trivial warped source which only such circumstances can make appear credible.

His name was Titus Oates, his religious background Non-conformist Baptist, his personal integrity non-existent. He claimed to have become reconciled, once, to Roman Catholicism. Quite likely he adopted this position in the hope of inveigling himself into the confidence of some genuine Roman Catholics, with the sole intention of twisting any 'equivocational' information that he could obtain about them into profitable blackmail. Such leering criminality would have fitted Oates' personality and ambition perfectly; "Faith! Here's an equivocator!" The fears of the time had created a happy hunting ground for such low-life as he. Somehow he was accepted into the Jesuit College at Valladolid in Spain, and then fetched up at St. Omers in 1678 where, it appears, he would have rubbed shoulders with some of the authors of the 'Opera of Tewdric'. From the conversation of his fellows, and no doubt by careful questioning of his own, he obtained the overall picture of the Louis XIV – Charles II treaty and its 'secret' clause to return England to Roman Catholic worship. Given the cynicism of our Merry Monarch, it is more than possible that Charles II had no basic intention to do anything more than keep the chests of golden *Louis d'ors* crossing the Channel under armed guard to fill his personal coffers, and so be independent of Parliament for much of his income. If Louis XIV was epitomising *La Gloire* in his rule, Charles was exploiting its grubby side, and cared not who suspected it so long as they they kept their suspicions to themselves and acknowledged him as King.

However, Oates, by whatever means he had employed to obtain the information, had discovered that the entire Jesuit administrative structure in England had met together to consult and confer on 24th April 1678. What he did not know was that it had met in the private rooms of Prince James, Duke of York, in Whitehall Palace! Had he been able to pose as a Jesuit a little longer he might have come by such information. But his conduct at St Omers was as offensive as his person and personality, and he was expelled in the summer of 1678, returning to England to make what he could of what he reckoned he knew. He found a 'useful fool', to use Lenin's terminology, in one Esrael Tongue, a crackpot hack journalist and pamphleteer who helped him invent and put together the details of The Popish Plot, "... a hellish plot to fire the City, raise the Catholics in Ireland, conquer England by French and Irish arms, massacre every Protestant who refused to recant, and murder the King ..."

Oates claimed falsely (obviously) to have been at the April meeting and thus able to go into tremendous detail about it. With Tongue's help he drew up a manuscript of 81 'revelations'; whole lists of 'conspirators', to which during the ensuing months he added all who dared to doubt his assertions, several score known English Jesuit Priests and their friends, and a few Catholic nobles for good measure. All who displeased this wicked, truthless creature were in danger. Even Samuel Pepys (the diarist and) Secretary to the Admiralty under Prince James (the necessary Roman Catholic connection) was gratuitously accused of harbouring treasonable intentions in relation to the Royal Navy. Oates was believed because he was plausible, given the prevailing atmosphere of distrust in the State. He needed no proof. He just painted the fears of the popular imagination, held up the picture, and heard it acclaimed as all too true. Terror was easily generated thereby.

Needless to add there were those who could have stopped him, but dared not do so. How would Charles have contrived to continue extracting money from Louis XIV if there had ceased to be a prospect of the re-conversion of England? How might he even have kept his throne had it become proven that he was a pensioner of a foreign power? Incredibly, Louis was also bribing many prominent English politicians to take a favourable view of French Continental ambitions, so these recipients of his bounty found it expedient to become vehemently anti-Roman Catholic lest their own affairs came under scrutiny. Even a certain Captain John Churchill, later Duke of Marlborough, the *Marbrouk* who in Queen Ann's reign would wreck French military ambitions, was receiving a pension from Louis as *de jure* Captain of one of the English regiments first sent by Cromwell and still serving in the French cause. Being Prince James' *homme d-affaires* in Court dealings with the French, usually centred upon obtaining more hard cash for Charles, he was not unknown at Versailles itself. In short, corruption was rife, and nothing was quite what it seemed. The sheer scale of this 'sleaze' meant that Oates was as likely as not to be somewhat right about some people, or various dealings and policies, no matter what he said. No-one initially was found to be sufficiently untainted to oppose his lies and bullying outright. Then the panic was increased by a fortuitous but strangely suggestive murder.

As was prudent in the circumstances, and no bad idea in any corporate setting, Oates had given a copy of his 81 'revelations' to a staid and trusted magistrate, Sir Edmund Berry Godfrey, in case Charles' Court and Royal Council contrived to 'lose' or otherwise suppress them. To public horror, and no doubt to Oates' private glee, Sir Edmund's corpse was found in a ditch below Greenberry Hill in (then) rustic Marylebone, marks of strangulation upon it, and his own sword thrust through his heart. Had the Roman Catholic massacre already started? Three unknown individuals, by curious coincidence bearing the names of Green, Berry and Hill, were duly tried for his murder and hanged; all of them were purportedly Roman Catholic.

Wonderful and strange ideas about this murder still abound. It has yet to be solved. Quite likely Berry Godfrey was walking alone and became the victim of foot-pads, who were not Green, Berry, and Hill. The whole business is cloudy and suspicious. And all who gave their evidence in the case were probably equivocating merrily anyway. Thousands attended Sir Edmund's funeral, the London train-bands (local militia) patrolled the streets at night, citizens of both genders armed themselves, and a vicious little blunt weapon dubbed 'The Protestant Flail' was mass-produced and profitably sold. It proved its usefulness in the political street-fighting of a year or so later.

No-one rates Sir Edmund Berry Godfrey as other than a good and honest man. He had a wide circle of friends and acquaintances, Roman Catholics amongst them, not unnaturally so in a closely knit social setting like London. One of them was Coleman, who was secretary to the Duchess of York, wife of Prince James. For years Coleman had been writing James' letters to Louis XIV as part of the process of extracting French money for Charles' private necessities. As long as this could be kept secret, it was just part of the political scenery. Once exposed, it was very obviously high treason. And Sir Edmund, out of friendship for Coleman, had told him of Oates' 81 'revelations', no doubt suggesting that he should be careful with whom he spoke and what he said. What Sir Edmund may, or may not, have known of the whole picture we may only speculate. But this draws us away from the tale of Tewdric.

The link with the Welsh Marches lies in another petty crook named William Bedloe, who was cashing in upon the prevailing panic in the land. Born in Chepstow, 1650, of a respectable background – his cousin William Kemeys, connected with an old Cavalier family, was High Sheriff of Monmouthshire in 1678 – Bedloe had received a good education and allied start in life. He was in London in 1670 and is known there to have become acquainted with Jesuits, although we must allow for such acquaintance with educated men to have begun whilst still part of some Chepstonian 'great household' in his youth. He is known to have travelled widely on the Continent with Jesuits during the 1670s, using fantastic aliases like 'Lord Gerard', 'Lord Newport', 'Lord Cornwallis', and in the process fantasising enough to become, willy-nilly, a casual confidence-trickster criminal.

He was in gaol for fraud in 1679 at any rate, and was granted his liberty by aiding Oates in his denunciations, specifically claiming to have heard during his imprisonment Berry, Green, and Hill admitting to the murder Sir Edmund Berry Godfrey. By sealing their fates and sending them to Tyburn gallows, he plausibly appears to have been shielding some other party or parties. One of Samuel Pepys' clerks, Atkins, was also for a time at risk from Bedloe's burblings, but sound detective work undertaken at considerable risk by Pepys himself cleared him. Overall Bedloe made Oates a poor witness, being keener to use the power of his fortuitous position to take small personal revenges of his own. He was, nonetheless, given a reward of £500 for his 'patriotism'. He subsequently married an Irish lady, lived "luxuriously", and died in Bristol in 1680, still ranting semi-incoherently about Jesuits. When calmer days returned, everyone dismissed him as a trivial nuisance. However, his early life might repay close examination and research. Was he a covert Roman Catholic? Had he Jesuit contacts at The Cwm or in some other Monmouthshire place? Was he even briefly at St Omers? What, if anything, may he have known about Coleman and Sir Edmund? Coleman, by accident as it is assumed, failed to burn a box of highly treasonable letters written in 1675, and these sent him to the gallows irrespective of Oates. But was Coleman seeking to turn King's Evidence and employ these same letters as proof of his patriotism amidst the hysteria? If so, whom had he in mind as his target traitor? Was Coleman, in effect, sacrificed by James?

These events were centred in London, but the rot had spread far, taking the panic and sudden zealousness in upholding the anti-recusant laws with it. Charles had an illegitimate son, the Duke of Monmouth, who was unquestionably a Protestant and, as such, was quickly adopted by the anti-Roman Catholic 'Whig' political faction in the land headed by the Earl of Shaftesbury. Shaftesbury had ambitions for himself, and was keen to use Monmouth as his political puppet. His basic idea, assuming that Charles produced no legitimate heir, was to have Prince James excluded from the succession and Monmouth crowned in his stead. Charles was well aware from James' efforts when governing as his Deputy in Scotland that he would make a very poor Monarch. Nevertheless he saw correctly greater dangers in the Crown's being in the 'gift' of the dominant political faction at the time of any reigning Monarch's death, and the whole edifice of Monarchy reduced to a political soap-opera accordingly. So he resisted the turmoil that Shaftesbury, using Oates, was whipping up against the Court, and knowingly sent many a good man to his death to preserve his own position and the due legal course of the Royal Succession. Caiaphas would have applauded him (cf St John's Gospel; 11. 49, 50). In mitigation of this *realpolitik* it is recorded that Charles specifically insisted that all those condemned should be dead from hanging before the disembowelling and dismembering commenced. Let us consider some of them.

St. Philip Evans. Born in Monmouth; date uncertain. Became a Jesuit 1665. Priested 1675, and sent to work in South Wales. A reward of £250 was offered for his capture in 1678. Arrested at Skier House in Glamorgan, and imprisoned in Cardiff Castle for five months, whilst

120

great difficulty was had in finding any witnesses to testify that they had seen him ministering as a priest. Eventually, tradition has it, a dwarf and a beggar woman provided the necessary evidence. Evans was a skilled tennis player and also a highly proficient harpist. The delay in his execution enabled him to gain a certain celebrity in both activities. Executed (hanged, drawn and quartered) 22July, 1679. On the scaffold he declared, "I die for God and religion's sake; and think myself so happy that if I had never so many lives, I would willingly give them all for such a good cause." Canonized by Pope Paul VI in 1970.

St. John Lloyd. Born in Brecon c1630. Entered the English seminary at Valladolid 1649. Priested 1653. Returned to Wales 1654. Arrested in Glamorgan 1678, and charged with having said Mass at Llantilio, Penrhos, and Triefor. Imprisoned in Cardiff Castle with Philip Evans, and executed with him (hanged drawn and quartered) on 22July.1679. Canonized by Pope Paul VI in 1970.

St. David Lewis. Born in Monmouthshire 1616 of Protestant Father and Roman Catholic mother. Educated at Abergavenny Grammar School and the Middle Temple. 1635, joined the household of the Comte Savage as tutor, and was received into the Roman Catholic Church in Paris, soon afterwards entering the English College in Rome. Priested in 1642. Became a Jesuit in 1644. Became Spiritual Director of the English College, but returned to Herefordshire in 1648 and worked there for the rest of his life. Centred his activity around Llanrothal farmhouse, which was sacked and its library taken to Hereford Cathedral when he was arrested in 1678. Imprisoned at Monmouth and tried at Usk for his priesthood, he was tied on to a horse by the stirrup straps, and taken to London for further questioning 1679. One may imagine the indignities and spites suffered by him on a journey of several days in each direction, in addition to the insults hurled at him in Court whilst his guilt was proven as required. On his return he was due to be hanged at Usk; but the official hangman fled. A convict was offered his freedom if he would take on the job, but he was stoned by by-standers and absconded at speed. Finally the local blacksmith was prevailed upon to carry out the sentence, which he did, making sure that Lewis was dead from hanging before the remaining savagery was performed. On the scaffold Lewis spoke at length in Welsh, summarizing his convictions and explaining why he was to suffer. Canonized by Pope Paul VI in 1970.

St. John Kemble. Born at St Weonards 1599. Educated at the English College in Douai, and Priested 1625. Returning home, he made his brother's house at Pembridge Castle his mission headquarters, and with help from Jesuits ministered over large areas of Herefordshire and Monmouthshire. Founded centres at the Llwyn, the Craig, Hilston, and Codangred. Ministered for 54 years altogether, until as part of operations associated with the Popish Plot he was arrested. Imprisoned at Hereford for three months. Sentenced to be hanged, drawn and quartered. Like David Lewis he was secured on horseback and conveyed to London for further questioning, additional pantomime being offered in the form of a promise of freedom, given his age, if he would reveal details of the non-existent Plot. When sent back to Hereford to be executed, the under-sheriff who came to escort him to the scaffold allowed him time to pray, and shared with him at his request a glass of wine and a final pipe of tobacco. He also ensured that Kemble was truly dead from hanging before allowing the sentence to proceed further.

St. Thomas Whitbread. Born in Essex 1618. Of considerable importance in the Jesuit community, his life is but sketchily known. He was Jesuit Provincial in the Low Countries and England in 1678, and was arrested as part of the Popish Plot hysteria, although ill with 'the plague' at the time. At some point in 1678 he had personally expelled Titus Oates from St Omers College, and refused him admission to the Jesuit order, on the grounds of Oates' ignorance, blasphemy, and sexual interest in young boys. Whitbread was able to confirm, and have his evidence supported by a deputation brought over from St Omers under a guarantee of safe conduct, that Oates was still resident at the College on 24th April 1678, and could not therefore, contrary to his own claim, have been at the Jesuit 'consult' in London; he carefully gave no more detail of whereabouts in London. Oates, however, was determined to have his revenge upon Roman Catholics in general and Whitbread in particular, and the evidence was dismissed as equivocation. Whitbread was hanged drawn and quartered at Tyburn in July 1679. Canonised in 1929.

The practice, actual or automatically assumed, of equivocation was turned against two young students from St Omers, **William Parry** and **Daniel Gifford** who were probably involved in writing the "Tewdric" opera. Gifford was arrested "... upon suspicion of being a priest ..." imprisoned in the Tower of London, and interrogated by the brutal Sir William Waller, son of a the Parliamentary general of the same name and far greater distinction who had conducted operations against Chepstow and its castle in 1648. Once again Tewdric's realm enters our picture. The youngsters were easily swayed to state that, in sworn obedience to their superiors in all matters, they would have to tell lies on their behalf if instructed to do so. At a stroke Waller had nullified all evidence from any source connected with St Omers College. Oates was safe, again, to lie and bully as he pleased.

Fourteen boys from St Omers had come to London to testify on Whitbread's behalf; by a minor miracle they all lived to tell of their experiences and return to St Omers. The verbal attacks upon these youngsters in the warped and rigged 'justice' of the Courts investigating Oates' non-existent Plot would have shaken them all considerably. In addition the nightly riot raging in the streets as the Whig political thugs, by then well under Shaftesbury's control, harassed all Roman Catholic 'traitors and suspects' to be persecuted as the result of that day's hearings, certainly imbued them with an all too justified impression of the heroism of Tewdric and Meurig in fighting off a pagan army.

The seeds for their dramatic piece had been well and truly sown. There is far more to their drama than is obvious at first sight; it borders on being an allegory of the Popish Plot itself.

11

Who's Who...?

Oates' fictitious 'Popish Plot' and its murderous consequences had thoroughly shaken the Roman Catholics in England and Wales. Shaftesbury and his Whigs laboured hard to keep the panic going in order to bring the Monarchy under their political control, using the Protestant Duke of Monmouth as their tool and puppet. Charles II was having none of it and eventually, 1681, called a Parliament at Oxford which he promptly dissolved, and ruled without one for the balance of his reign. He died in 1685. James Duke of York succeeded him as James II, and at once proceeded to commit practically every political blunder imaginable by advancing Roman Catholics to various important Offices of State, thereby raising once more all the fears and suspicions associated in the popular mind with Papists, and risking a return to the terrors of 1679. Monmouth, in exile in Holland in 1685, tried to claim the Crown and landed in the West Country. The wholesale national support he needed was at that time lacking, however, and his brave little force of West Countrymen was slaughtered in battle on the Levels of Sedgemoor. Monmouth fled, but was soon arrested and executed.

By continuing to behave as an absolute monarch after the totalitarian pattern of Louis XIV, James had alienated almost all shades of opinion at every level in the land by 1688, however. The Protestant Dutch William of Orange, married to Mary, James' sister, accepted the (treasonable) offer of the Crown, by John Churchill amongst others, disembarked an army at Torbay, and did little for a week or so in order to give the deserted James II a respectable period in which to quit The Throne and flee the country. At the second attempt – the first having been thwarted by some indignant and probably vengeful Protestant fishermen – James was permitted to succeed. Thus a bloodless revolution was achieved, to everyone's sincere relief. The one great legacy of James reign, in fact, had been the definitive Act of Habeus Corpus, aimed against James' arbitrary inclinations, and requiring all arrested persons to be produced in court within a few days to be formally charged and made aware of the legal proceedings proposed against them. So much for the period 1678 – 1688 from the English point of view.

This decade firmly settled the foundations of the British Constitution, and it was during the earlier part of these tremendous years that "Sanctus Tewdricus sive Pastor Bonus" ("*St. Tewdric or The Good Shepherd*") was written, refined, had some music fitted to it, and was performed at St Omers College. Prof. Whitehead and Dr. Leech, along with others whose researches have touched upon the piece, have achieved wonders in suggesting its several authors from amongst a cloud of aliases adopted for their safety when, as they assumed, they would be ministering to English and Welsh Roman Catholics upon British soil. The two main themes of the work are the necessity of opposing evil, resorting to arms if circumstances so require it, and of magnanimity and reconciliation thereafter. The Christian ideals of loving God before all, and affording one's neighbour the same degree of consideration and courtesy as one would expect, indeed, require, of him /her are plainly displayed by the action. One thinks of Tewdric's battle for the safety of his people, and Meurig's thirty years of peaceful rule thereafter. This is consistent with our main traditions.

Other episodes, especially the gory business with Arthurus carrying the head of the recently decapitated Fridericus in a bag, along with a desecrated crucifix to his own compatriots/allies as some sort of peace-offering, come from elsewhere. One thinks of the ancient Celtic habit of head-hunting. It is not a theme which resonates with thoughtful speculation and detective work upon incomplete sources still available to us in the twenty-first century. Some of the extras may be from traditions so far unidentified; some may be the original melodramatic output of young minds thoroughly shaken by their treatment in God's name by Oates' lies and judicial murders, along with Shaftesbury's baying, jeering, intimidating political mobs in London; others may have some deeper, subtler significance in Jesuit thinking of the period. Given that the perspective of the years yields us a clearer idea of events 1678-1688 than any one person is likely to have had at that time, although many would have known more small details than ever we can lay claim to, let us consider the characters of "Sanctus Tewdricus sive Pastor Bonus" and try and match them in this context with their seventeenth century historical counterparts. Do we have a drama, or an allegory, or some of both, in short?

Tewdricus A king who, after an active military youth, has settled to quiet his soul in religious contemplation as a hermit in a wild and beautiful place. He aids his successor, his son Meurig, to fight off foes and protect his Crown and Realm, his victory granting peace for thirty years, and giving Meurig the unofficial title of 'Father of Wales'.

Alias – Charles II, whose father was beheaded, who fought at Worcester and hid up an oak tree, which did not change the colour of its leaves as in "Tewdricus", but gave him sylvan protection. We may remark, however, that the green leaves of the oak at Boscobel manor amongst which Charles II is reputed to have hidden whilst Cromwell's ironsides sought him after his defeat at Worcester, here wither; a victor's laurel which becomes a crown is presented to him instead. Very symbolic, we cannot but choose so to see it. Having secured his throne in 1660, he was quite content to live, in semi-indolence with his mistresses, upon Louis' bribes to re-convert his realm. Once stirred to action by 'Saxons' – ie Oates and Co. – he reasserts himself in 1681 at Oxford, and makes secure his Crown for his successor, James II.

Identity between history and drama secure enough.

* * *

Mauricus (given its Welsh phonetic values, ie 'My-rick-iss' the name is even more exact) King by inheritance, and son of Tewdric. Donates the Manor of Mathern, where Tewdric is buried, to The Church. Rules as a Christian and is applauded as a good king.

Alias – Meurig. This is James II, heir to Charles II, and a good Roman

Catholic. If "Tewdricus" dates from around 1680, his political ineptitude as a king is not yet on show.

Identity between history and drama highly probable.

* * *

Otho One of the villains of the piece. His vainglorious boasting and general offensiveness suggest a vile creature. He does not appear to have been killed in the Welsh counter-attack of Tewdricus and Mauricus.

Alias – Titus Oates. In tune with the Oates/Otho naming. The historical Otho was one of the Four Emperors, and reigned for 95 days during that twelve-months AD 68/69 according to Suetonius. After a dissolute youth when he was one of the yobbish gang headed by the young Nero, Otho was notorious for ingratiating, wheedling, manipulating, and worming his amoral way into positions of power and influence, even briefly to the Imperial Throne itself. This would fit the aspiring Oates perfectly. He survived 1681, was imprisoned by James II on his accession and, since shameless perjury did not carry a death sentence at law, was repeatedly whipped and harshly treated in gaol in the undoubted hope that such abuse would kill him. It did not. James did not reign long enough to achieve this purpose, and under William-and-Mary Oates was awarded some sort of naval chaplaincy and a pension, eventually, of £300 pa. He died in 1705, still bewailing what he saw as the ill-fortune and injustices inflicted upon him throughout his life.

Identity between history and drama a good fit.

* * *

Sigertus Another 'Saxon' villain. Desecrates a crucifix, and stabs Arthurus in the hands – Christ's wounds? – when rebuked. Finally surrenders to Tewdricus, who spares his life. In direct contrast to this saintly goodness, he stabs Arthurus. His death is not recorded in the drama's synopsis.

Alias – the Earl of Shaftesbury (formerly Ashley Cooper, one of Charles II' s initial 'cabal', derived from the initials of the names of five individuals in his close confidence at the start of his reign). A brilliant politician, and the main force of the 'Whig' radical faction in Parliament. His aim was to limit the Monarch's powers, and in view of what Louis XIV was achieving as an absolute monarch in France, he was worthy in ensuring that Parliament should have control over such matters as finance and the size of the military. He was strongly anti-Papist /Absolute Monarchy, and was unperturbed about stirring up a London based mob-rule to support his aims. One of these was to seat the guileless royal bastard, Monmouth, on the throne, as we have mentioned already. He died in 1683; which may help narrow the date for the writing and performance of "Tewdricus", perhaps 1680 – 82?

Identity between history and drama adequately certain.

* * *

Arthurus A Christian defector to the heathen Saxons, apparently Mauricus' brother. Mocked for objecting to the crucifix desecration episode. Beheads Fridericus, and returns with his head and the desecrated crucifix in a bag, to a chance family reconciliation. Treacherously stabbed by Sigertus.

No ready historical – drama identity perceived.

* * *

Malcolmus Portrayed as Welsh, peacefully intentioned, dithering, fearful of Ulfadus, whom he eventually kills in seeming panic, and is still alive at the end of the drama. He is an enigma both to the plot and dramatic necessity. For that matter, so is Ulfadus.

No ready historical – drama identity perceived.

In conclusion we still retain the bardic tale of Tewdric and the Christian traditions associated with his place in history. He defended his Faith, his people, and their way of life from attack by something alien and abhorrent to them. He himself was killed by a fatal wound resulting from an 'angon', a type of Anglo-Saxon lance, thrown by an enemy already in retreat. Thirty years of peace resulted from his stand and, as it turned out, sacrifice. This was how his contemporaries saw it and celebrated it. A later age knew his story, and drew parallels between it and the events of their own times.

Perhaps we do the same, in so far as we examine the world in which we live and find in the human stories underlying its politics and standards of behaviour, some features akin to the times of The Popish Plot as well as the late sixth century ... or thereabouts. Humanity endures. Faith sustains it. We are all part of life's drama.

Envoi

In St. Tewdric's church at Mathern a small plaque has been appended to Bishop Godwin's memorial outlining the circumstances of St Tewdric's death. It reads, "A stone coffin was found whilst the chancel was under repair in 1881 beneath this tablet, where it was replaced at the completion of the the work together with the bones that it contained."

REQUIESCAT IN PACE

Acknowledgements

I would like to thank the following people whose comments and advice have been helpful in the production of this book: Miles Bailey (The Choir Press), John Gale, Peter Holman, Valerie Holman MPV, Dr. Mark Lewis PhD, Martin Lusmore, Pat Osley, Jan Pain, Prof. Maurice Whitehead, Canon Andrew Willie.

Bibliography

Alcock – Leslie; 'Arthur's Britain' (Penguin)

Ashe – Geoffry; 'The Quest for Arthur's Britain' (Paladin)

Barber – Chris; 'More Mysterious Wales' (Paladin)

Bede; 'A History of the English Church and People' (Penguin Classics)

Brewer – Richard J. 'Caerwent Roman Town' (Cadw; guidebook)

Care-Evans – Angela; 'The Sutton Hoo Ship Burial' (British Museum Press)

Coxe – Rev'd; William; 'Monmouthshire'

Crummy – Philip; 'City of Victory' (Colchester Archaeological Trust)

'Current Archaeology' 'Current World Archaeology' Various. (Current Publishing)

Davies – E T Rev'd; 'A History of the Parish of Mathern' (local publication by Mathern Parochial Church Council)

Farley – Julia } 'Celts; art and identity'
Hunter – Fraser } ' (British Museum & National Museum of Scotland)

Flatman – Joe; 'Ships and Shipping in Mediaeval Manuscripts' (British Library)

Farmer – D H; 'The Oxford Dictionary of Saints' (Oxford University Press)

Frodsham – Paul; 'Cuthbert and the Northumbrian Saints' (Golden Age of Northumbria Project)

Gerrard – James; 'The Ruin of Roman Britain' (Cambridge University Press)

Gildas; 'De Excidio Britanniae' Books 1 & 2, translator, J A Giles (Dodo)

Glob – P V; 'The Bog People' (Paladin)

Goodman – Martin; 'Rome and Jerusalem' (Penguin)

Grant – Michael; 'The World of Rome' (Cardinal)

Gwilym-Jones – Rev'd D B; 'The Parish Church of Sant Clydawg' (local publication by Parochial Church Council)

Leech – Peter)
                    } ; 'New light on music and musicians at St Omers English Jesuit College 1658–1714'
Whitehead – Maurice ⌋   [Paper in 'Tijdschrift van de Koninklijke Vereniging voor Nederlandse Musziekgeschiedenis' volume LXVI – 1 / 2 2016]

Newman – Paul; 'Lost Gods of Albion' (The History Press)

[Nordbok] 'The Lore of Ships' (Nordbok)

[Ordnance Survey] 'Map of Roman Britain' 3rd edition. 'Britannia in the Dark Ages' 2nd edition: maps.

Roderick – Alan; 'The Folklore of Gwent' (Cwmbran Community Press)

Sin – David; 'The Roman Iron Industry in Britain' (The History Press)

Suetonius; 'The Twelve Caesars' (Penguin Classics)

Stenton – Sir Frank; 'Anglo-Saxon England' (Oxford University Press)

Sturluson – Snorri; 'The Prose Edda' (Everyman)

Tacitus; 'On Britain and Germany' (Penguin Classics)

Trevelyan – G M; 'England under the Stuarts' (Pelican)

Waite – John; 'To Rule Britannia' (The History Press)

Walters – Bryan; 'The Ancient Dean and the Wye Valley' (Thornhill Press)

Wilkins – Alan; 'Roman Artillery' (Shire Archaeology)

Wright – Stephen K; 'Manuscript of *Sanctus Tewdricus*; Rediscovery of a "Lost Miracle Play" from St. Omers.' [Paper published by the Biographical Society of the University of Virginia: 'Studies in Bibliography', Volume 42 (1989)]

About the Author

The author was born during latter stages of World War II. His early life and education were based around the old Roman town of Colchester, which possibly influenced his subsequent decision to read History at the University of Bristol.

Upon graduation he entered the Senior Civil Service and worked for a while in London, but the air pollution of the capital obliged him to move to a fresh air zone on medical grounds. For the next 32 years he derived income and subsequent pension from the Post Office in Wales, a period much enlivened by a couple of secondments he engineered to off-shoots of The Welsh Office.

Upon settling in Mathern in 1970 he came upon St Tewdric's tomb in the village church, later officiating there and at other places of worship around the Diocese of Monmouth as a Lay Reader; he is also a bell-ringer, and organist of very last resort.

He is married – over 40 years ago and continuing – with two adult children now making their own ways in the world.

His interest in history continues, supported by membership of The Chepstow Society, Shirenewton Local History Society, and Friends of Colchester Archaeological Trust.

He is happy to sing with any choir which is short of a bass, lectures periodically on historical and psychical research themes, and often ends up with a posse of eves-droppers when conducting friends and visitors around local castles and other ancient places.

By way of physical activity he enjoys walking amidst the local wondrous scenery.

Index

www.ingramcontent.com/pod-product-compliance
Lightning Source LLC
Chambersburg PA
CBHW050823090426
42738CB00020B/3458